Constructing Staircases, Balustrades & Landings

WILLIAM P. SPENCE

Sterling Publishing Co., Inc.
New York

Library of Congress Cataloging-in-Publication Data
Spence, William Perkins-, 1925.
    Constructing staircases, balustrades & landings / William P. Spence.
        p. cm. -- (Building basics)
    Includes index.
    ISBN 0-8069-8101-6
    1. Staircases--Design and construction I. Title. II Series.
TH5667.S64 2000
694'.6--dc21   00-037291

Designed by Judy Morgan
Edited by Rodman Neumann

1   3   5   7   9   10   8   6   4   2

Published by Sterling Publishing Company, Inc.
387 Park Avenue South, New York, N.Y. 10016
© 2000 by William P. Spence
Distributed in Canada by Sterling Publishing
c/o Canadian Manda Group, One Atlantic Avenue, Suite 105
Toronto, Ontario, Canada M6K 3E7
Distributed in Great Britain and Europe by Cassell PLC
Wellington House, 125 Strand, London WC2R 0BB, England
Distributed in Australia by Capricorn Link (Australia) Pty Ltd.
P.O. Box 6651, Baulkham Hills, Business Centre, NSW 2153, Australia
Printed in China
All rights reserved

Sterling ISBN 0-8069-8101-6

Contents

1. PRELIMINARY PLANNING   4

   Locating the Stair 4 • Codes Related to Stair Design 8 • Types of Stairs 10 • Parts of a Stair 12

2. DESIGNING A STAIR   14

   Building Codes 14 • Calculating the Unit Rise & Run for a Straight Stair 18 • Reading a Stair Drawing 21 • Architectural Woodwork 25

3. FRAMING STAIRWELLS   26

   Framing a Straight Stair Stairwell Opening 26 • Building the Stairwell 29 • Adding a Stair to an Existing House 33

4. STRAIGHT STAIRS WITH NOTCHED STRINGERS   36

   Stringer Requirements 36 • Laying Out the Stringer 39 • Installing the Stringers 41 • Cutting & Installing the Skirtboard 44 • Installing Treads & Risers for Carpeted Stairs Using Notched Stringer 48 • Hardwood Treads & Risers on Notched Stairs 50 • How to Miter the Skirtboard or Riser 53 • How to Miter the Stringers 55

5. STAIRS USING HOUSED STRINGERS   60

   Laying Out a Housed Stringer 60 • Assembling the Housed Stair 66 • Installing the Assembled Stair 71

6. L-SHAPED & U-SHAPED STAIRS & LANDINGS   72

   Building Landings 72 • Framing the Landing 77 • Turning Stairs with Winders 82 • Manufactured Stairs 88

7. CURVED & SPIRAL STAIRWAYS   92

   Spiral Stairways 97

8. INSTALLING THE BALUSTRADE   100

   Installing the Starting Newel 104 • Mechanical Connectors 108 • The Balustrade 113 • Installing a Post-to-Post Balustrade 115 • A Simple Variation 127 • Installing an Over-the-Post Balustrade 129 • Handrails for Closed Stairs 137

9. OPEN-RISER STAIRS   138

   Designing the Stair 138 • Laying Out the Stringer 139 • Assembling the Stair 141 • Manufactured Open-Riser Stairs 142

10. DISAPPEARING STAIRS   146

   Folding Disappearing Stairs 146 • Installing the Stair 151 • Sliding Disappearing Stairways 155

METRIC EQUIVALENTS   156

INDEX   157

CHAPTER 1

Preliminary Planning

A stair is an important part of the trafficway in your house. Stairs plus the halls give you access to space on several levels and a means of exiting the house from upper floors. Adequate space must be allowed on the floor plan so the stair can effectively route the traffic flow within the building. In addition to providing access to other levels, a stair can be designed so it is a major design feature. An attractive stairway off the foyer or living room can provide a grand entrance into that area (1-1).

The slope of the stair must meet building codes but also enable it to fit comfortably within the floor plan. One way to do this is to change the shape of the stair (1-2). A straight stair with open balustrades makes a room appear larger because you can see through into the next room (1-3). Consider the use of open balustrades for at least part of the stairway.

LOCATING THE STAIR

If you are designing a new house, you have considerable freedom when locating a stair. First, consider how it is to be used. For example, a stair to a basement usually is not a major item but needs to be located so it is easily accessible from the more frequently occupied areas of the house. Also, beauty may not

1-1 This curved stairway provides a dramatic grand entrance for the foyer.

Courtesy Designed Stairs, Inc. 1-877-4Stairs

1-2 This stair is in a U-shape using a landing to change the direction. The open balustrade on the stairway and the landing on the second floor provide an attractive architectural feature.

1-3 The open balustrade on this straight stair is not only attractive but opens up the rooms where it is located.

necessarily be a factor. A stair to the second floor usually provides access to bedrooms and baths. Since this is a high traffic area it needs to be rather centrally located and provide easy access from first-floor areas. On the second floor it is the way down and should be located so each room has short and easy access to it.

When locating a stair, consider its relationship to such other features as any doors, to rooms, or to the front entrance. Crowding it up against the front entrance can create a real problem because of congestion and a conflicting door or doors that may block the stair (1-4).

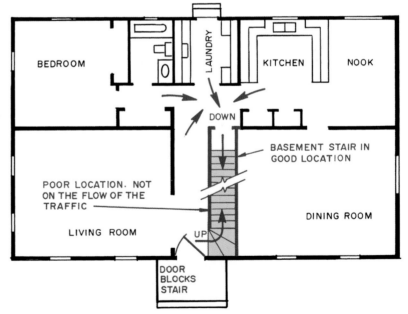

1-4 The stairway access is blocked by the open front door, making access difficult and bothersome. The stair to the basement is located directly below, saving floor space. It is well located because it is accessed from several areas of the house.

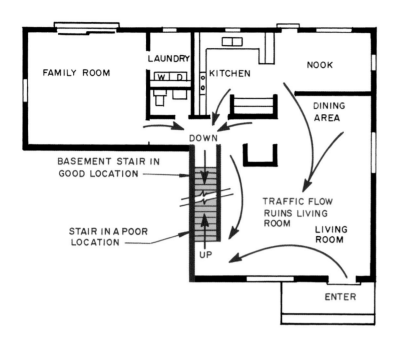

1-5 This plan makes the living room into a hall with all the traffic to the second floor passing through it. It ruins the room as a place for conversations and pleasant meetings.

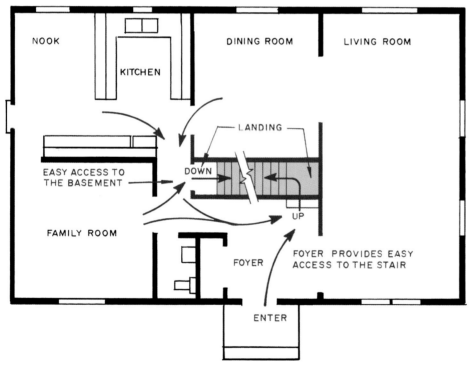

1-6 An entrance foyer provides easy access to the stairway to the second floor, and if it has an open balustrade creates an attractive architectural feature.

Stairs located on an outside wall rob you of the opportunity to have a number of windows, thus reducing natural light and any view. They also require you to walk through a room to reach them and are not as readily accessible from other parts of the house as they might be (1-5).

The large entry foyer in 1-6 provides an excellent means for moving traffic to the second-floor stair and for providing easy access to the other rooms. Not everyone can afford to devote this much space to a foyer, however, and a centrally located stair is more often used (1-7). The centrally located stair tends to divide the house into two sections but is often in the most economical location. If it can have the basement stair below it, this provides maximum use of the floor area it occupies. Observe how this will influence the traffic on the second floor.

As you plan your stair location consider taking advantage of having one or both sides of the stair open. This will help reduce or eliminate the tunnel feeling of a closed stair. An open stair is very attractive and also makes the adjoining room or rooms seem somewhat larger (1-3).

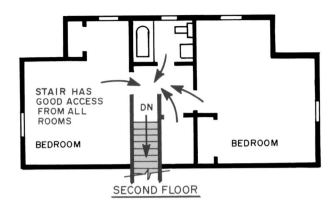

STAIR HAS GOOD ACCESS FROM ALL ROOMS

BEDROOM

DN

BEDROOM

SECOND FLOOR

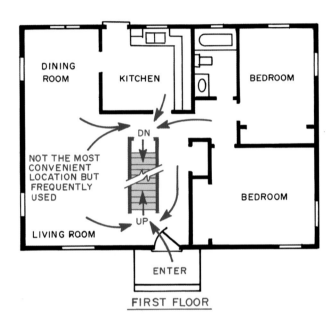

DINING ROOM

KITCHEN

BEDROOM

DN

NOT THE MOST CONVENIENT LOCATION BUT FREQUENTLY USED

BEDROOM

UP

LIVING ROOM

ENTER

FIRST FLOOR

1-7 The centrally located stair provides adequate access from both the first and second floors, but it is not the best traffic solution. It is widely used, however.

The basement stair is often located below the stair to the second floor. This lets you use the floor space occupied by the stair to serve two stairways. Therefore, if you plan to do this you must consider access to the basement stair at the same time you locate the stairway to the second floor. The same technique is used for three-story houses. The third-floor stair can be built above the second floor stair (**1-8**).

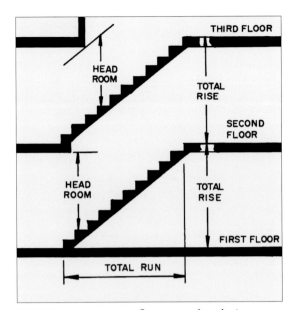

THIRD FLOOR

HEAD ROOM

TOTAL RISE

SECOND FLOOR

HEAD ROOM

TOTAL RISE

FIRST FLOOR

TOTAL RUN

1-8 You can conserve floor space by placing one stairway below another.

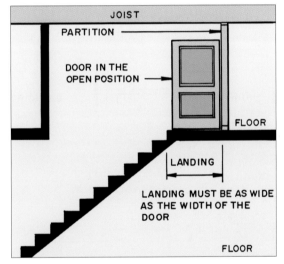

JOIST

PARTITION

DOOR IN THE OPEN POSITION

FLOOR

LANDING

LANDING MUST BE AS WIDE AS THE WIDTH OF THE DOOR

FLOOR

1-9 When a stair has a door opening onto it, the stair must have a landing at least as wide as the width of the door.

It is important to know that any stair that is entered directly from a door-as is typical for basement stairs-must have a landing that is at least as wide as the width of the door (**1-9**). Check your local code to verify the required width of the landing.

CODES RELATED TO STAIR DESIGN

You must be certain your stair is designed to meet local building codes. The codes are prepared to set standards that are determined necessary for a safe stair. If the rise is too high or the tread too narrow, it could cause an injurious fall.

While codes may vary a little they in general have the same basic set of requirements. Following are specifications typically found in many codes. Consult your local codes so your stair will pass inspection.

RISE & RUN

The rise and run in a stair must be the same for the entire length of the stair. Codes permit a small variance which can be caused by cutting, but try to keep it to 1/16 inch—about the width of a saw kerf. A 3/16-inch difference may pass inspection, but try to work closer. The commonly used **maximum riser** is 7 inches. However, some codes permit risers to be 7¾ to 8½ inches if the occupancy of the building is less than 10 people. The commonly used **minimum riser** is 4 inches,

Unit Rise	Unit Run	Approx. Degrees of Slope	Total 2 risers plus 1 unit run = 24" to 25"
6⅝"	11⅜"	30°-30'	24⅝"
6¾"	11¼"	31°-30'	24¾"
7"	10½"	33°-35'	24½"
7½"	9½"	38°-15'	24½"

1-11 Examples of acceptable rise and run proportions.

The commonly used unit run is 11 inches. However, some codes permit it to be 10 inches, if the occupant load is less than 10 people (**1-10**). Check your local code. While these sizes can vary slightly depending on the code, a rule of thumb to find a comfortable combination is that the sum of 2 risers plus 1 tread without the 1in nosing should not be less than 24 inches or more than 25 inches, Some examples are shown in **1-11**.

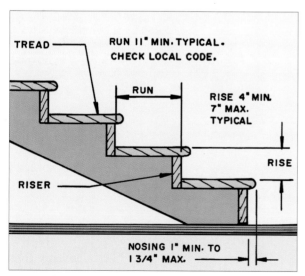

1-10 These are the typical riser and tread requirements for stairs in residences. Check your local building code for requirements for your house.

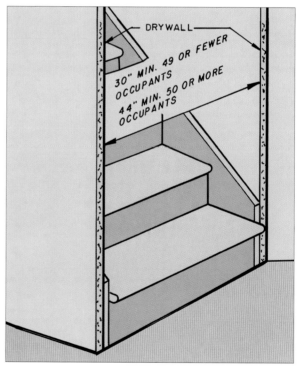

1-12 The minimum stair width is regulated by the number of occupants in the building who use the stair. Check your local code.

STAIR WIDTH

Residential stairs must be at least 36 inches wide if the building has an occupancy load of 49 people or less. This would apply to single-family and multifamily residences. If a building has an occupancy load of 50 or more, the stair must be 44 inches wide (**1-12**).

HANDRAILS

Handrails are carefully regulated by local building codes. They are very important because they prevent falls. The handrails must be securely fastened to the wall framing. Standard handrails and hanging devices are widely available.

Following are typical code specifications:

Stairs less than 44 inches wide must have a handrail on one side. Those that are 44 to 88 inches wide must have a handrail on each side. If a stair is over 88 inches wide, a third handrail is needed in its center (**1-13**).

Handrails are to be located 30 to 38 inches measured vertically above the tread and have at least 1½ inches clear space between the wall and handrail.

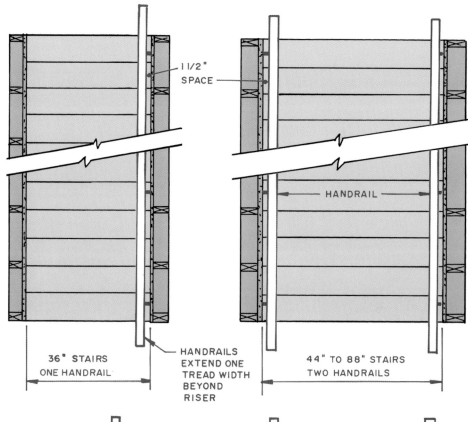

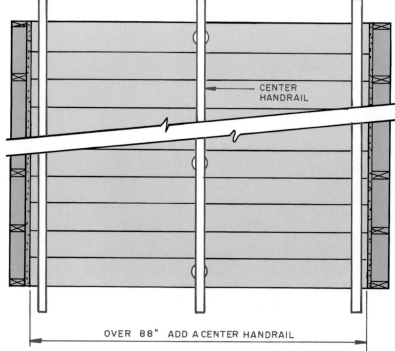

1-13 Codes regulate the use of handrails based on the width of the stairway.

They should not extend more than 3½ inches into the required stair width. In addition they must run continuously the entire length of the stair and extend 12 inches beyond the top riser and one tread width beyond the bottom riser. The handrail should be 1½ to 2 inches in cross-sectional areas and have all smooth edges (**1-14**).

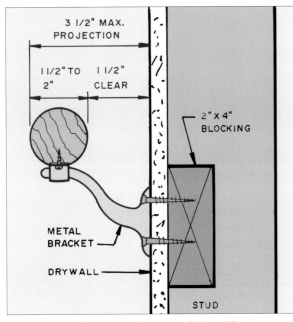

1-14 Handrails mounted on a wall should not extend more than 3½ inches clearance between the wall and handrail. Allow at least 1½ inch clearance between the wall and the handrail.

1-15 The space between balusters is regulated by code. Codes typically allow a maximum of 4 inches, This prevents children from pushing their heads between the balusters and getting caught.

SLOPE OF A STAIR

The stair should be designed so it is on an angle of 30 degrees to 35 degrees. Angles to 40 degrees can be used if the rise and run limits are met.

LANDINGS

Landings should be as wide or wider than the stair. The width in the direction of travel need not be more than 4 feet. Review Chapter 6 for more information.

BALUSTERS

The spacing between balusters is generally limited by code to 4 inches. The actual spacing should permit two balusters to rest on each tread (**1-15**). Review Chapter 8 for more information.

TYPES OF STAIRS

The commonly used stairs include straight, L-shaped, U-shaped, and circular.

A straight stair may be a single unbroken flight or have a landing about halfway up their length (**1-16**). The landing extends in the same direction of the stair and must be the same width. A landing is a horizontal break in a stair that makes it into two shorter straight flights. A landing is required if the height of the stair is 12 feet or more.

An L-shaped stair consists of a landing and two short flights of straight stair. It makes the stair turn 90 degrees (**1-17**). There are examples in Chapter 6.

A U-shaped stair also has a landing, but the landing is twice the width of the stair (**1-2**). It makes the stair turn 180 degrees (**1-18**).

A variation of the L-shape and U-shaped stair uses winders in the landing area (**1-19**). Winders are triangular-shaped treads, each rising one step above the one below it as they turn the stair in another direction. They are more dangerous to use and are avoided when possible. Construction details and photos are shown in Chapter 6.

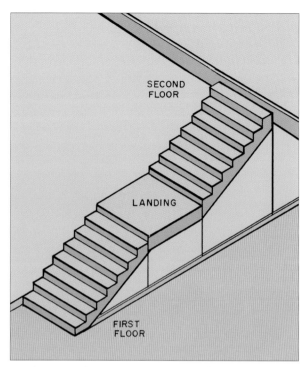

1-16 A straight stair is the easiest to build. It may have a landing partway up and must have a landing if the total rise is 12 feet or more.

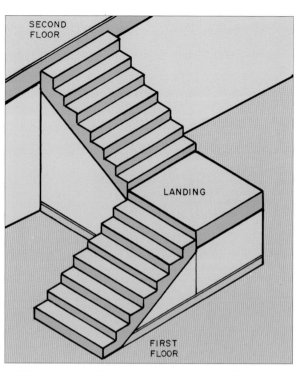

1-17 An L-shaped stair lets you change the direction of the stair, allowing you to possibly fit it into the floor plan where a straight stair run would be too long.

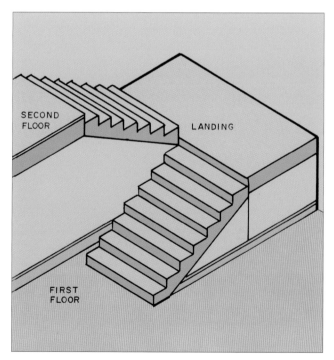

1-18 A U-shaped stair turns the stair 180 degrees, using a large landing.

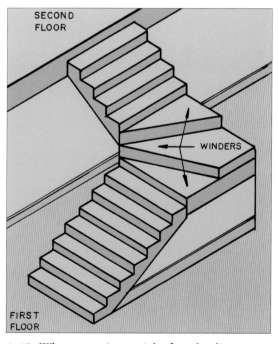

1-19 When space is too tight for a landing on an L-shaped stair, winders can be used—thus reducing the square feet required on the floor plan.

A circular stair rises in the form of a helix. As it turns it moves the riser and treads around a large central newel post. The circular stair is decorative and requires less floor space than other types. However, it is harder to use and very difficult to move furniture up and down (**1-20**). Additional examples are shown in Chapter 7.

<h2 style="text-align:center">PARTS
OF A STAIR</h2>

Each part of a stair has a specific name and while these will vary somewhat in different parts of the country the following are typical.

The terms "stair" and "stairway" are generally used to describe an assembly of treads, risers, landings, balustrades, stringers, and other parts. Technically the completed assembly is a staircase. The opening in the floor through which the stair is built is the **stairwell opening** (**1-21**). See Chapter 3 for more information.

Courtesy Designed Stairs, Inc. 1-877-4Stairs

1-20 Circular stairs provide access to another level and require the least amount of floor space. They are more difficult to use than the other types.

1-21 The stairwell is an opening built in the floor through which the stair will be built.

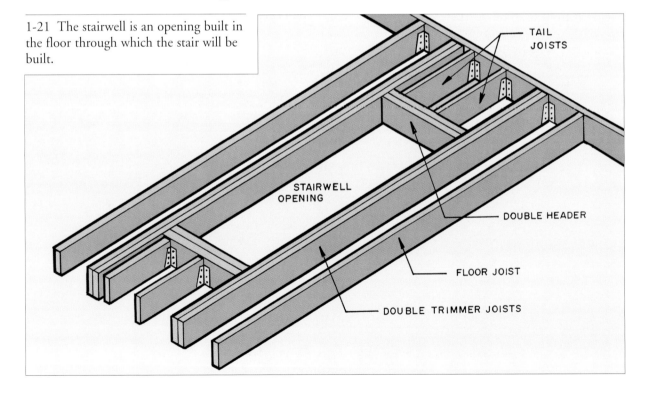

TAIL JOISTS

STAIRWELL OPENING

DOUBLE HEADER

FLOOR JOIST

DOUBLE TRIMMER JOISTS

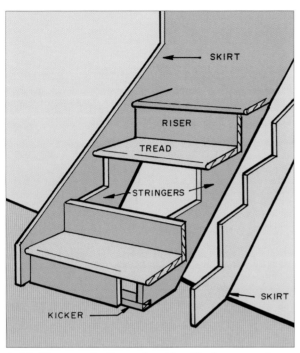

1-22 Terms typically used to identify the parts of a stairway.

1-24 The assembled balustrade provides protection from falling off the side of the stairway and is by itself a thing of beauty.

The terms used to identify the parts of a stair are used in **1-22**. The staircase has steps consisting of a **riser** and a **tread**. The diagonal members supporting the steps are called **stringers** or **carriages**. The trim used to cover the stringers and provide a finish along the wall is a **skirtboard**.

Terms used to identify balustrades are shown in **1-23**, including the balusters, newel posts, and the handrailing. **Balusters** are vertical members that run between the handrail and the tread, supporting the handrail. **Newels** are large posts to which the handrails are attached. A **starting newel** is at the bottom

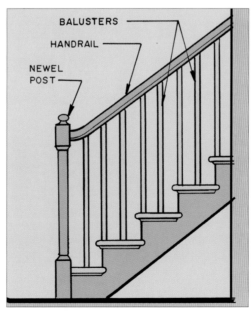

1-23 Balustrade terminology.

of the stair. If you have a landing, you will also have a **landing newel** and, if there is a turn in the stair, an **angle newel**. The **handrail** is supported by the **newel posts** and is the part that you rest your hand on as you use the stair.

The balustrade in **1-24** illustrates the beauty of the installation and the protection it provides for those using the stairway. (See Chapter 8 for more information.)

Designing a Stair

2-1 If space is tight, you may not be able to design the long staircase you might prefer, but often creative and interesting solutions can be found.

Courtesy Designed Stairs, Inc. 1-877-4Stairs

Several factors must be considered during the design process. First, you must observe the requirements set in the local building codes. Next, you need to measure the actual floor-to-floor height and ascertain the amount of floor space available. If space is tight, you may not be able to design the long, easily traversed stair that you would prefer (2-1).

You will have to develop a compromise between the space available and what the codes permit. It is fine to exceed the codes on the width, landing, and handrail requirements. If possible, this will produce a more acceptable stair. Codes give minimum and maximum requirements on tread and riser sizes, stair width, landing sizes, and other features.

BUILDING CODES

The local building code regulates the design and construction of stairs. Most communities adopt one of the model codes and sometimes add additional regulations. These codes tend to be used in various regions of the United States, so stairs built in California might be different from stairs built in, e.g., New York State.

Several of the national code organizations recently joined together, with input from representatives of professional and trade organizations and representatives of the building trades, developed a national code in which the requirements are the same over the entire United States. This will mean that a stair designed and built in California will meet the same requirements as one built in New York State after both states adopt this new code. This new code is the *International Residential Code.* As it is adopted by local governments, the existing codes related to stairs will have some changes.

As you design and build a stair, you must observe the regulations in your local building code. The sizes referred to in this book are typical of those currently used, however.

RISE & RUN

The **unit rise** s the vertical height of one step and the **unit run** is the horizontal size of one step, as shown in **2-2**. The actual tread board is equal to the unit run plus the nosing that extends beyond the finished riser board. Typically the maximum unit rise allowed is 7¾ inches and the minimum unit run is 10 inches,

A decision on the size of the rise and run affects all other aspects of the stair. The **total run** is the horizontal distance found by multiplying the unit run by the number of runs. If you make the stairwell this long, you will have the maximum headroom. However, you can get the minimum headroom, 6 feet 8 in, required by codes and have the stairwell a bit shorter than the total run as shown in **2-2**.

The **total rise** is the height of one rise multiplied by the number of risers (**2-2**). When you are figuring the total rise, you must also take into consideration the situation from one floor to the next as it relates to the subfloor and any finished flooring to be used.

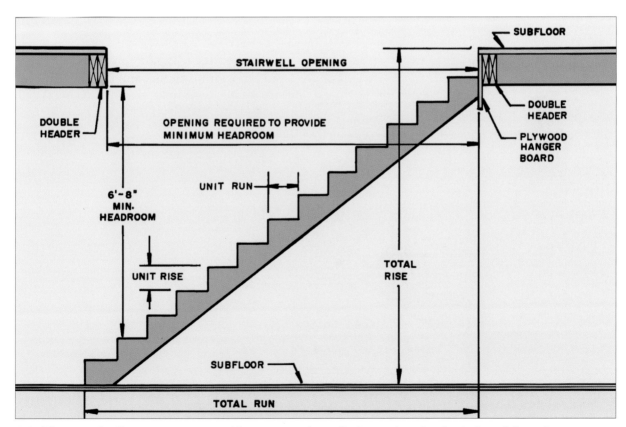

2-2 These are the factors you must consider as you make preliminary plans for the design of the stair.

If the lower and upper floors have finished flooring-carpet, solid wood or a laminated product-that is the same thickness, the subfloor-to-subfloor dimension will be the same as finished floor to finished floor, as shown in **2-3**.

If the stringer rests on the subfloor, you will need to add the thickness of the finished floor to the height of the first riser, as shown in **2-4**, to get the height of the first riser on the stringer.

If one floor, say, a basement, will not have a finished floor but the floor above does, add the finished floor thickness to the subfloor-to-subfloor distance (**2-5**).

If the two floors have finish coverings that differ in thickness, add the thickness of the upper flooring and subtract the thickness of the lower flooring to get the finished-floor-to-finished-floor distance (**2-6**). When the stringer rests on the subfloor add the thickness to the riser height, as shown in **2-4**.

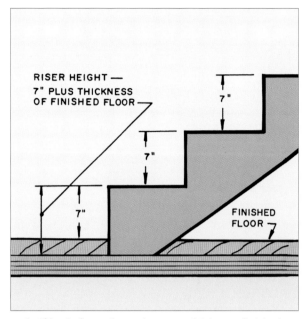

2-4 If both floors have the same-thickness finished flooring and the stringer rests on the subfloor, you need to add the thickness of the flooring to the size of the first riser.

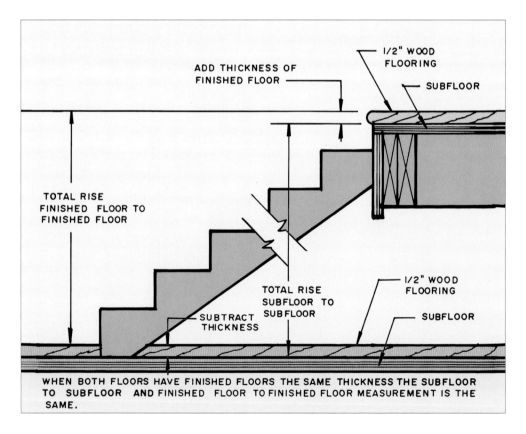

2-3 When both floors have the same-thickness finished flooring and the stringer rests on top of the finished floor, the total rise is the same as the subfloor-to-subfloor height.

2-5 When only one floor has a finished floor covering add its thickness to the subfloor-to-subfloor height.

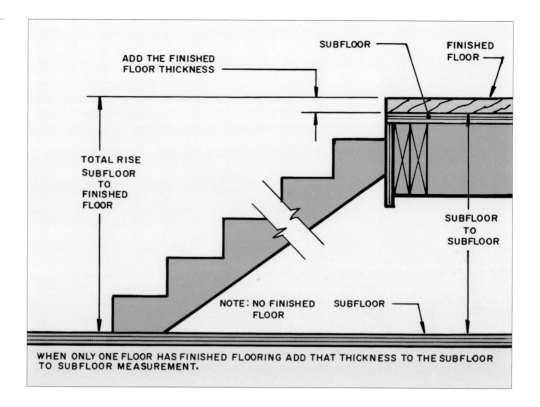

ADD THE FINISHED FLOOR THICKNESS

SUBFLOOR

FINISHED FLOOR

TOTAL RISE SUBFLOOR TO FINISHED FLOOR

SUBFLOOR TO SUBFLOOR

NOTE: NO FINISHED FLOOR

SUBFLOOR

WHEN ONLY ONE FLOOR HAS FINISHED FLOORING ADD THAT THICKNESS TO THE SUBFLOOR TO SUBFLOOR MEASUREMENT.

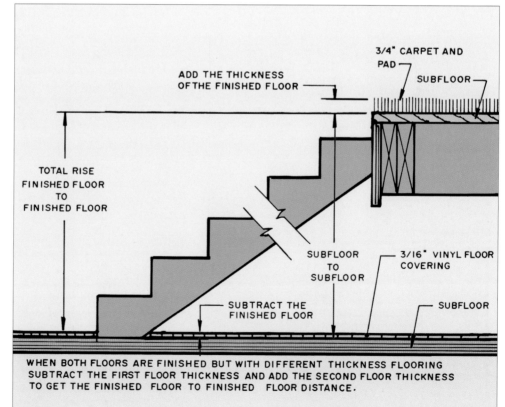

ADD THE THICKNESS OF THE FINISHED FLOOR

3/4" CARPET AND PAD

SUBFLOOR

TOTAL RISE FINISHED FLOOR TO FINISHED FLOOR

SUBFLOOR TO SUBFLOOR

3/16" VINYL FLOOR COVERING

SUBTRACT THE FINISHED FLOOR

SUBFLOOR

WHEN BOTH FLOORS ARE FINISHED BUT WITH DIFFERENT THICKNESS FLOORING SUBTRACT THE FIRST FLOOR THICKNESS AND ADD THE SECOND FLOOR THICKNESS TO GET THE FINISHED FLOOR TO FINISHED FLOOR DISTANCE.

2-6 If both floors have finished covering but they are of different thickness, subtract the thickness of the lower floor and add the thickness of the upper floor.

DESIGNING A STAIR

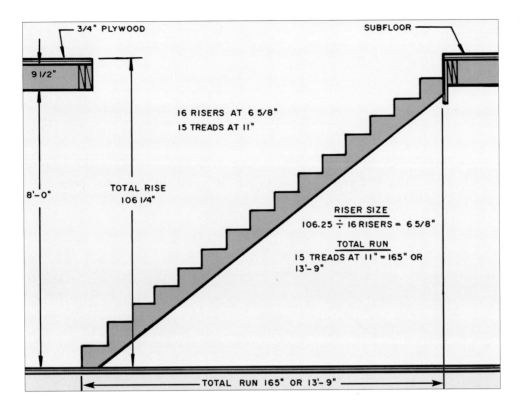

3/4" PLYWOOD

9 1/2"

SUBFLOOR

16 RISERS AT 6 5/8"
15 TREADS AT 11"

8'-0"

TOTAL RISE
106 1/4"

RISER SIZE
106.25 ÷ 16 RISERS = 6 5/8"

TOTAL RUN
15 TREADS AT 11" = 165" OR
13'- 9"

TOTAL RUN 165" OR 13'- 9"

2-7 You adjust the number of risers until their height meets the code. As you do this, the number of treads is also changed—which establishes the total run of the stair.

CALCULATING THE UNIT RISE & RUN FOR A STRAIGHT STAIR

Begin by figuring the **unit rise.**

Divide the **total rise** by 7 inches, which is a comfortable rise and smaller than the allowed maximum of 7¾ inches. This will give a number of risers and usually a little left over.

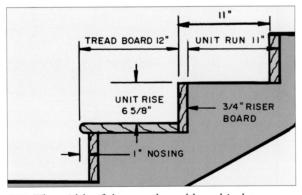

TREAD BOARD 12"   11"
UNIT RUN 11"

UNIT RISE
6 5/8"   3/4" RISER
BOARD

1" NOSING

2-8 The width of the actual tread board is determined by the unit run plus the size of the nosing.

In the example shown in **2-7**, the total rise was 106¼ inches. This division gives 15 risers at 7 inches and has 1¼ inches left over. If you prefer a slightly smaller rise and want to be certain to meet the code, then divide the 106¼ inches by 16 risers, from which you will find that the riser size is 6⅝ inches, providing a total rise of 106 inches, which is close enough to the total rise.

Most codes specify a minimum tread width of 10 in, though it could be smaller under certain conditions. If we use the 11 inches tread (unit run)—of which there are 15—the **total run** is 165 inches or 13 feet 9 inches (**2-7**).

The **unit run** is the distance from the face of one riser to the face of the next riser. The actual tread board will be wider because it has a rounded nosing extending beyond the face of the riser board below—usually 1 inch but not more than 1⅛ inch. In our example if we use a 1 inch nosing, the tread board will be 12 inches wide (**2-8**).

If you prefer to have a lower rise, rework this problem using it. This will produce additional risers and unit runs (treads) and will increase the length of the total run. Check to be certain you have enough floor room on the plan for the longer stair.

ON-SITE CALCULATIONS

If the stairwell has already been built and you have to design a stair to fit the total height available and meet the code, you will have to:

1. Measure the actual stairwell opening,
2. Measure the actual total rise,
3. Allow for finished flooring, and
4. Try to meet local codes.

Make a sketch of what you have similar to that in 2-7. Then begin by dividing the total rise with a convenient unit rise and reach a solution like the one shown in 2-7.

If the total run calculated is so long you will not have the minimum headroom clearance, select a larger unit rise and refigure the unit, so that the stair fits the stairwell opening. Hopefully you will not need to rebuild the stairwell framing. Remember, you need to check to be certain there is room on the floor plan for a longer stair.

CHECK FOR HEADROOM

Codes typically require a minimum of 6 feet 8 inches headroom on stairs in residences running between floors and 6 feet 4 inches on basement stairs. This is regulated by the amount of floor area on the second floor that you can allow for the stair. If this is equal to the total run, you have no problem (2-9).

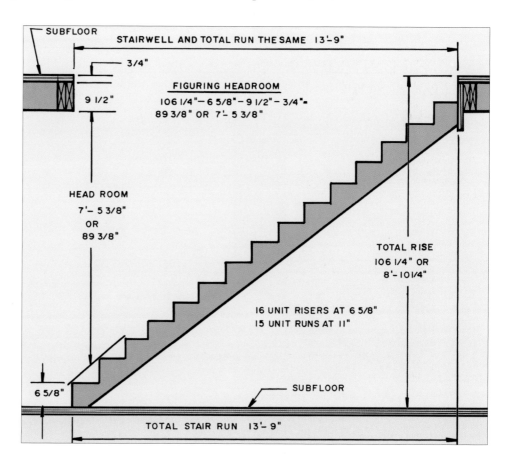

2-9 When the stairwell and total run are the same, you get considerable headroom.

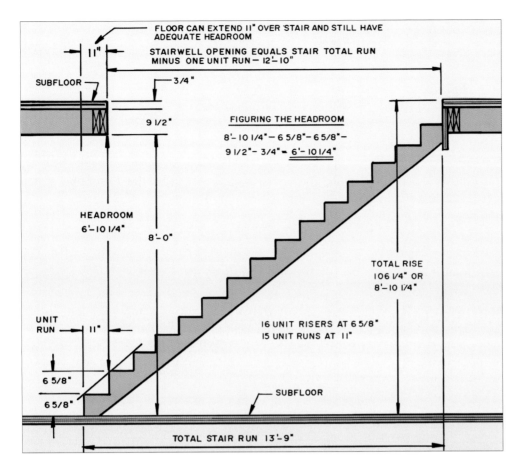

FLOOR CAN EXTEND 11" OVER STAIR AND STILL HAVE ADEQUATE HEADROOM

11"

STAIRWELL OPENING EQUALS STAIR TOTAL RUN MINUS ONE UNIT RUN — 12'-10"

SUBFLOOR

3/4"

9 1/2"

FIGURING THE HEADROOM

8'-10 1/4" — 6 5/8" — 6 5/8" —

9 1/2" — 3/4" = 6'-10 1/4"

HEADROOM
6'-10 1/4"

8'-0"

TOTAL RISE
106 1/4" OR
8'-10 1/4"

UNIT
RUN

11"

16 UNIT RISERS AT 6 5/8"
15 UNIT RUNS AT 11"

6 5/8"

6 5/8"

SUBFLOOR

TOTAL STAIR RUN 13'-9"

2-10 When you shorten the stairwell length, you change the headroom of the stair. You can figure the headroom available by deducting the stair unit rise. In this example the floor was extended one unit run over the end of the stair.

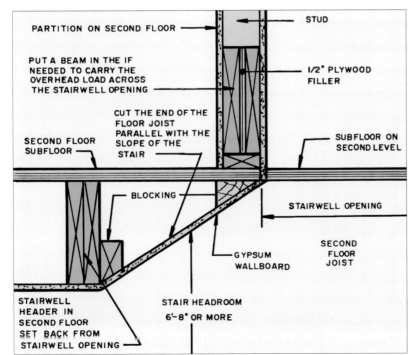

PARTITION ON SECOND FLOOR

STUD

PUT A BEAM IN THE IF NEEDED TO CARRY THE OVERHEAD LOAD ACROSS THE STAIRWELL OPENING

1/2" PLYWOOD FILLER

CUT THE END OF THE FLOOR JOIST PARALLEL WITH THE SLOPE OF THE STAIR

SECOND FLOOR SUBFLOOR

SUBFLOOR ON SECOND LEVEL

BLOCKING

STAIRWELL OPENING

GYPSUM WALLBOARD

SECOND FLOOR JOIST

STAIRWELL HEADER IN SECOND FLOOR SET BACK FROM STAIRWELL OPENING

STAIR HEADROOM
6'-8" OR MORE

2-11 You can gain some headroom by recessing the stairwell header and slanting the end of the floor joists. If the cantilevered floor area will be under load, install a beam in the partition across the stairwell opening.

If the amount of floor area on the second floor that you can allow for the stair has to be tightened up a bit, the second floor will encroach over the stair as shown in **2-10**, reducing the available headroom. If you still have at least 6 feet 8 inches of headroom, you are fine, but seven feet is much better.

If your design is below code, you will have to refigure the stair, change the second floor plan, or cut the end of the over-hanging floor joist, as shown in **2-11**. This works fine if this sloping surface is in a closet. If the cantilever is large you will need to add blocking and other structural members.

READING A STAIR DRAWING

On the architectural drawings the architect will usually prepare a stair drawing and give the desired unit rise and unit run for the stair. The framers will prepare the stairwell according to this plan.

The plan views of stairs in **2-12** are typical of what is usually shown on architectural drawings. When you arrive to build the stair, check what has already been framed against the architect's drawings. Then refigure what it will take to build a stair in the opening provided and the floor space available. This is a check on what was proposed and what was built.

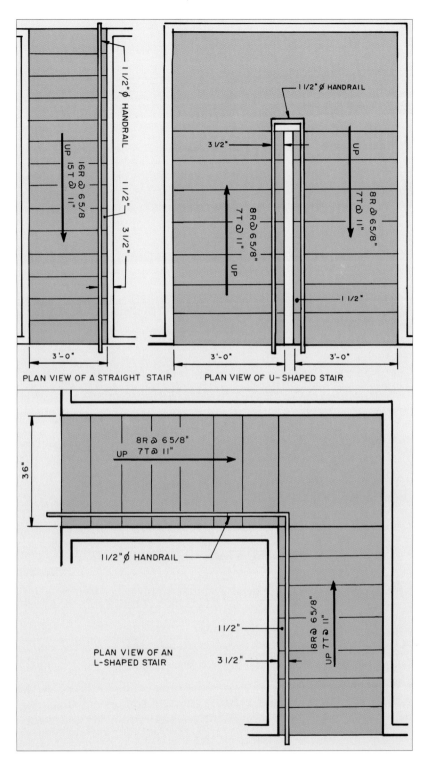

2-12 Typical stair details as found on architectural drawings. Before you start constructing, you will have to measure the actual total rise and run of the existing stairwell as well as ceiling height, and design the stair for the existing conditions. The rise and run may differ from the drawing.

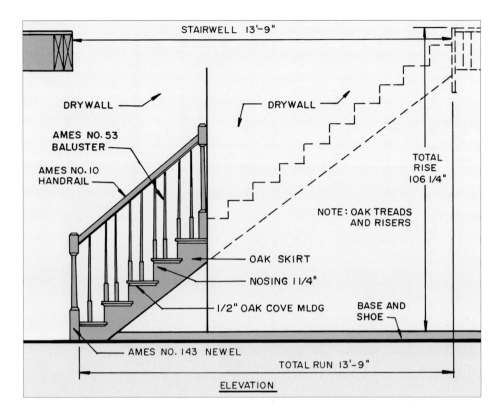

STAIRWELL 13'-9"

DRYWALL

DRYWALL

AMES NO. 53 BALUSTER

AMES NO. 10 HANDRAIL

TOTAL RISE 106 1/4"

NOTE: OAK TREADS AND RISERS

OAK SKIRT

NOSING 1 1/4"

1/2" OAK COVE MLDG

BASE AND SHOE

AMES NO. 143 NEWEL

TOTAL RUN 13'-9"

ELEVATION

2-13 This is a typical stair drawing found on architectural working drawings when an elevation is used to present information about the balustrade.

Sometimes a side view, similar to **2-7**, is also given. An example of a stair with a balustrade is in **2-13**. The elevation view gives the details about the balustrade

PLANNING
AN L-SHAPED STAIR

An L-shaped stair can descend through a square or rectangular-shaped opening in the floor. If you are designing the stair as the plans are drawn, you have the freedom to decide the height of the landing. Generally it is placed half-way between floors.

Begin by calculating the unit rise and unit run that you want to use for the stair. Then establish the **landing height** by selecting the number of risers you want to reach it. Going from the landing to the upper floor will require the rest of the risers. Remember, the landing takes the place of one tread.

The width must meet code, which is typically 36 inches, If possible plan the stair a little wider, such as 38 to 40 inches,

The width of the landing should be the same as the stair width. The length of the landing can be longer than the width, but on a 3 foot stair not over 4 feet.

To find the **stairwell length** you need to add the width of the lower flight plus the total run of the upper flight plus any offset necessary between the flights (**2-14**).

The **width of the stairwell** containg the lower flight is equal to the lower total run, any offset, plus the width of the landing (**2-15**).

Remember, the landing is not necessarily always in the center of the stair. As the number of risers in each flight changes, the size of the stairwell changes too.

Also remember, the code specifies a minimum width of 36 inches clear, so be certain to add the thickness of any drywall on the adjoining walls.

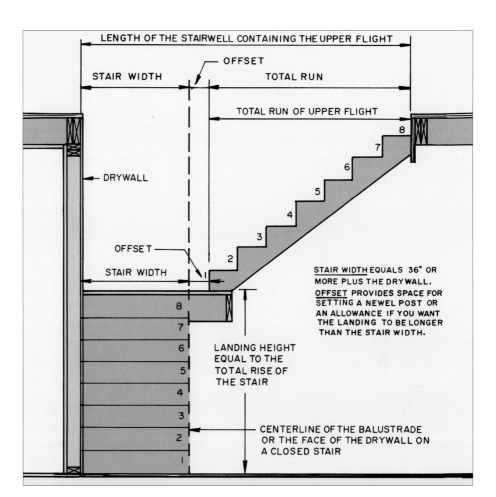

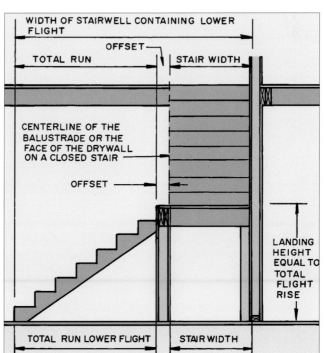

2-14 The length of the stairwell for the side containing the upper flight of an L-shaped stair includes the width of the lower flight, any offset, and the total run of the upper flight.

2-15 The width of the stairwell opening for an L-shaped stair containing the lower flight includes the width of the upper flight, any off-set, and the total run of the lower flight.

PLANNING
A U-SHAPED STAIR

The factors discussed for planning an L-shaped stair apply to the U-shaped stair. A plan view is shown in **2-16**. Review the layouts in **2-14** and **2-15** for additional information. These factors include calculating the unit rise and unit run that you want to use for the stair, establishing the **landing height** by selecting the number of risers you want to reach it, and remembering that the landing takes the place of one tread.

The stair width must meet code, which is typically 36 inches, If possible plan the stair a little wider, such as 38 to 40 inches,

The width of the landing should be twice the stair width plus any offset. The length of the landing can be longer than the width, but on a 3 foot stair not over 4 feet.

To find the **width of the stairwell opening** you need to add the width of the landing to the total run of the lower flight plus any offset necessary between the flights.

The **length of the stairwell opening** is equal to the width of both flights plus any offset.

Again, remember that the landing is not necessarily always in the center of the stair; as the number of risers in each flight changes, the size of the stairwell changes; and allow for the thickness of any drywall on the adjoining walls.

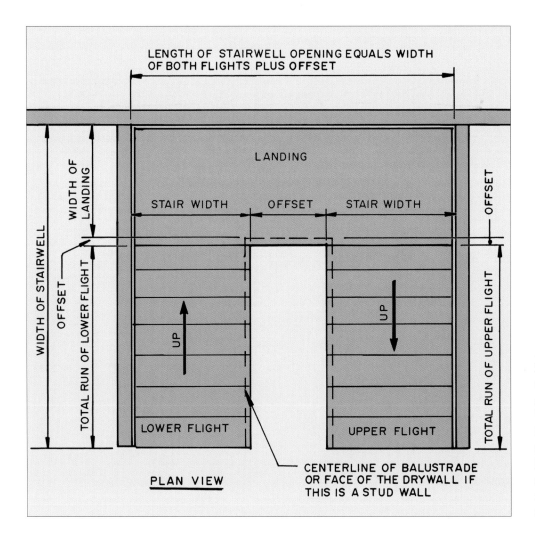

2-16 The size of the stairwell opening for a U-shaped stair includes the sizes of the landing, any offsets, and the total run of each flight.

ARCHITECTURAL WOODWORK

As you plan the stair you must also make decisions relating to the materials to be used. These would involve things such as the quality of the treads, risers, and stringers. The balustrade is the dominant architectural feature, so the choice of quality balusters, newels, handrails, and accessories is important. Two organizations that work to keep the quality of architectural woodwork products high are the Architectural Woodwork Institute and the Stairway Manufacturers Association.

THE ARCHITECTURAL WOODWORK INSTITUTE

The mission of the Architectural Woodwork Institute (AWI) is to establish quality standards through research and testing, and provide education through seminars, workshops, publications, and networking. It maintains a certification program to produce quality products in architectural woodwork, and to monitor, disseminate and influence governmental and environmental information and issues.

Membership includes many of the dominant associations from the various areas associated with construction. Many manufacturers participate in the AWI Quality Certification Program and show the AWI seal on the products and in their brochures.

In the AWI publication, *Architectural Woodwork Quality Standards,* Section 800 is devoted to stair work and railings.

THE STAIRWAY MANUFACTURERS ASSOCIATION

The Stairway Manufacturers Association is a broad-based association having members from the stair parts manufacturing companies, stair builders, installers and millwork distributors, and dealers. It works with members in the industry to write standards, perform testing, and promote products that ensure the growth of the industry. It is actively involved with the development of the model building codes and prepares standards to ensure that design and installation criteria meet or exceed the minimum standards set by the codes.

ADDITIONAL INFORMATION
Architectural Woodwork Institute
1952 Isaac Newton Square West
Reston, VA 20190

Stairway Manufacturers Association
P.O. Box 1363
Poplar Bluff, MO 63902

Framing Stairwells

The **stairwell** is an opening in the upper floor through which the stair is built. The actual framing used can vary depending upon the circumstances, but the following examples are typical of those frequently used. The designing and sizing of the stairwell are discussed in Chapter 2. Generally the stair builder will arrive on the job and find the stairwell framed by the crew building the wood framing. The stair contractor should check it to be certain it is the correct size and is built properly so that the stair constructed through it will be adequately supported (**3-1**).

Metal joist hangers are widely used to make the needed connections. They are strong and easy to install. Some connections can be made by end-nailing, as discussed later in this chapter.

FRAMING A STRAIGHT STAIR STAIRWELL OPENING

The size of the stairwell opening is found as the stair is designed. What you must do is leave the rough opening sized to accept the finished stair and the wall finish material. The width likewise must allow at least 36 inches minimum clearance between the finished walls or from a wall and the handrail of the balustrade.

The framing for a stair parallel with the floor joists is shown in **3-2**. Notice that the trimmer joists on the sides and the headers on each end are doubled. If a stairwell is longer than 10 feet, you should provide additional support. This is especially important if the doubled joists have to support a load from above, such as a load-bearing partition. If you have any doubt increase the support. Unusual situations may require the services of an engineer.

Courtesy Designed Stairs, Inc. 1-877-4Stairs

3-1 The stair builder must check to be certain that the designed stair will be adequately supported by the stairwell opening constructed by the framing crew.

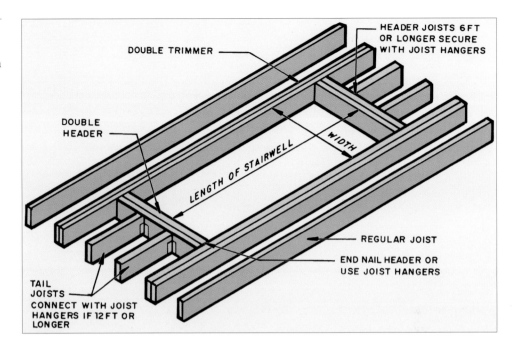

3-2 Typical stair-well framing when it runs parallel with the floor joists.

DOUBLE TRIMMER

HEADER JOISTS 6FT OR LONGER SECURE WITH JOIST HANGERS

DOUBLE HEADER

LENGTH OF STAIRWELL

WIDTH

REGULAR JOIST

END NAIL HEADER OR USE JOIST HANGERS

TAIL JOISTS CONNECT WITH JOIST HANGERS IF 12 FT OR LONGER

The details for framing the stairwell when the opening is perpendicular to the joists are shown in **3-3**. Since the header is serving as a beam and carries the ends of a number of floor joists, it may need to be tripled or, if the span is greater than 10 feet, a partition may have to be built beforehand. If there is any doubt, as always, it is best to consult an engineer.

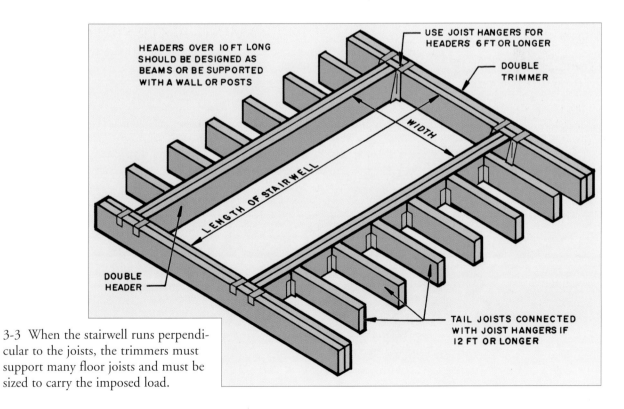

HEADERS OVER 10 FT LONG SHOULD BE DESIGNED AS BEAMS OR BE SUPPORTED WITH A WALL OR POSTS

USE JOIST HANGERS FOR HEADERS 6 FT OR LONGER

DOUBLE TRIMMER

WIDTH

LENGTH OF STAIRWELL

DOUBLE HEADER

TAIL JOISTS CONNECTED WITH JOIST HANGERS IF 12 FT OR LONGER

3-3 When the stairwell runs perpendicular to the joists, the trimmers must support many floor joists and must be sized to carry the imposed load.

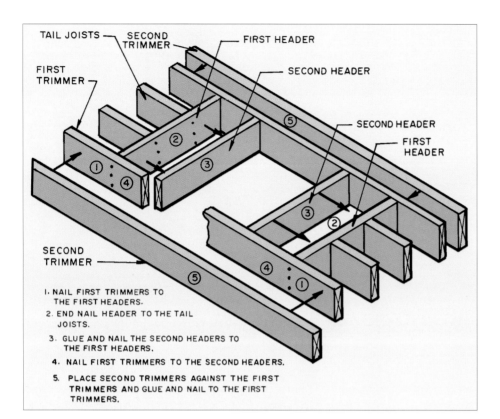

TAIL JOISTS — SECOND TRIMMER — FIRST HEADER

FIRST TRIMMER — SECOND HEADER

SECOND HEADER — FIRST HEADER

SECOND TRIMMER

1. NAIL FIRST TRIMMERS TO THE FIRST HEADERS.
2. END NAIL HEADER TO THE TAIL JOISTS.
3. GLUE AND NAIL THE SECOND HEADERS TO THE FIRST HEADERS.
4. NAIL FIRST TRIMMERS TO THE SECOND HEADERS.
5. PLACE SECOND TRIMMERS AGAINST THE FIRST TRIMMERS AND GLUE AND NAIL TO THE FIRST TRIMMERS.

3-4 This is how to assemble a narrow stairwell with glue and nails.

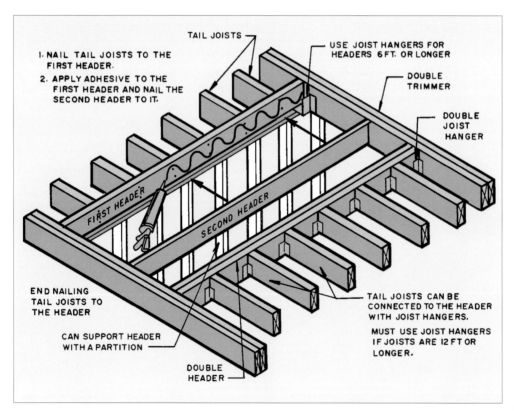

1. NAIL TAIL JOISTS TO THE FIRST HEADER.
2. APPLY ADHESIVE TO THE FIRST HEADER AND NAIL THE SECOND HEADER TO IT.

TAIL JOISTS

USE JOIST HANGERS FOR HEADERS 6 FT. OR LONGER

DOUBLE TRIMMER

DOUBLE JOIST HANGER

FIRST HEADER

SECOND HEADER

END NAILING TAIL JOISTS TO THE HEADER

CAN SUPPORT HEADER WITH A PARTITION

DOUBLE HEADER

TAIL JOISTS CAN BE CONNECTED TO THE HEADER WITH JOIST HANGERS.

MUST USE JOIST HANGERS IF JOISTS ARE 12 FT OR LONGER.

3-5 This is how to frame the stairwell when the stair runs perpendicular to the floor joists. You can end-nail in some cases, while others require the use of joist hangers.

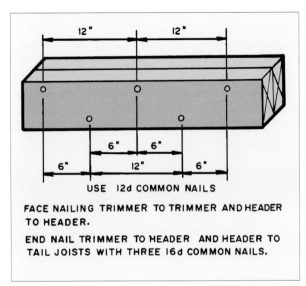

12" 12"

6" 6"

6" 12" 6"

USE 12d COMMON NAILS

FACE NAILING TRIMMER TO TRIMMER AND HEADER TO HEADER.

END NAIL TRIMMER TO HEADER AND HEADER TO TAIL JOISTS WITH THREE 16d COMMON NAILS.

3-6 Typical nailing recommendations for framing the stairwell.

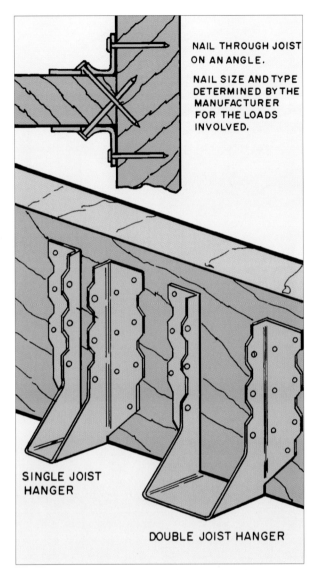

NAIL THROUGH JOIST ON AN ANGLE.

NAIL SIZE AND TYPE DETERMINED BY THE MANUFACTURER FOR THE LOADS INVOLVED.

SINGLE JOIST HANGER

DOUBLE JOIST HANGER

3-7 Metal joist hangers provide a rapid and strong method for joining joists, headers, and trimmers. Observe the manufacturer's recommendations relating to the type and size of hangers and the nails to use for various loads.

BUILDING THE STAIRWELL

The stairwell is built as the floor is framed. Consult the architectural drawings so you locate it exactly where it is planned. While this may interrupt the floor framing plan, an accurate location is important.

When you reach the location of the stairwell, double or triple the trimmer joists as required. If you plan to end-nail the headers to the trimmers, nail them through one trimmer and then install the second trimmer (3-4). Never nail headers through a double trimmer; you will not get enough nail in the header to hold it securely under load. If the stair is perpendicular to the joists, one of the long headers can be end-nailed to the joists or hung with a double joist hanger. The butting floor joists can then be end nailed through this header and the second long header glued and nailed to the first header, forming a beam (3-5).

Recommended nailing patterns and nail sizes are in **3-6**. Check your local code to confirm these recommendations.

Many carpenters prefer to use metal joist hangers. The trimmer joists and headers are hung with double joist hangers. The tail joists and butting floor joists use joist hangers (3-7). When you use metal joist hangers you can install the trimmers and then the headers, followed by the joists.

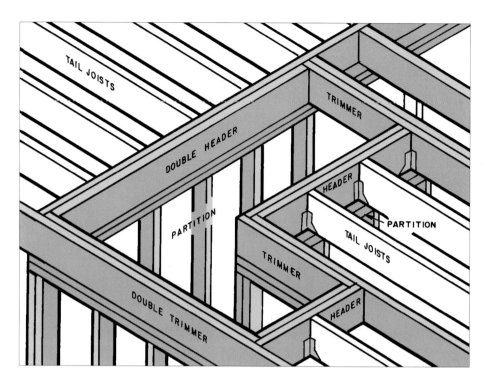

3-8 Typical framing for an L-shaped stair when the long side runs perpendicular to the floor joists. The trimmers and headers need to be designed to carry the planned floor loads above them.

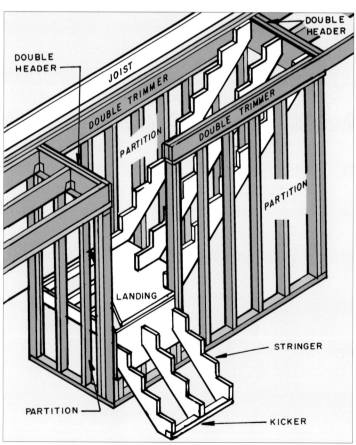

STAIRWELLS FOR L-SHAPED & U-SHAPED STAIRS

Framing the stairwell opening for L-shaped and U-shaped stairs can vary, depending on the design of the stair. Typical framing details are shown in **3-8, 3-9,** and **3-10.**

In **3-8** and **3-9** are typical framing details for an L-shaped stair. The double trimmers or headers need to be supported by a partition below and be designed as beams to carry the overhead load or be supported by columns.

The framing for a U-shaped stair is much like that shown for the L-shaped stair (**3-10**). It has long trimmers and headers that need support as described for the L-shaped stair.

3-9 Typical framing for an L-shaped stair when the long side runs parallel with the floor joists.

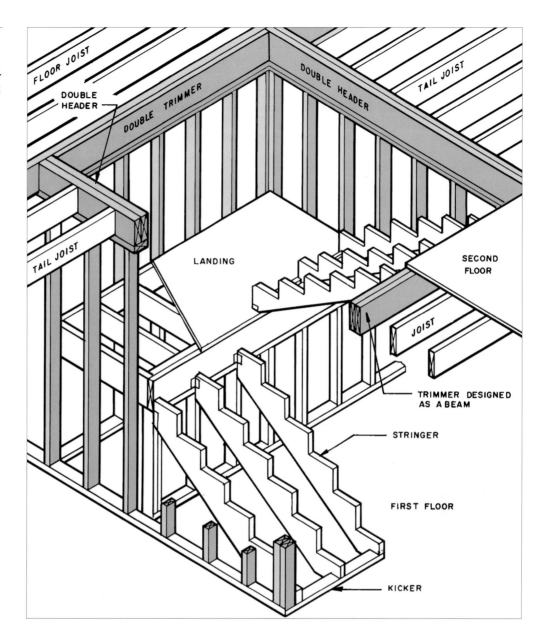

3-10 Typical framing for a U-shaped stair. Other framing plans are used depending upon whether the stair is closed or has some open portions with an exposed balustrade.

FRAMING A STAIRWELL
WITH I-JOISTS

I-joists are wood structural members made with an oriented strandboard web and laminated veneer lumber flanges (3-11). They serve the same purpose as wood joists in floor construction.

3-11 I-joists have laminated veneer lumber flanges and oriented strandboard webs. They can span long distances when used for residential construction.

One way to frame the stairwell with I-joists is shown in **3-12**. Consult the I-joist manufacturer's instructions before proceeding.

Typical construction details are shown in **3-13** and **3-14**. You should consult the manufacturer's installation instructions and the local building code before selecting the method of assembly.

The trimmer joists can be doubled I-joists with a two-inch-thick solid or laminated wood filler when the stairwell opening runs parallel with the floor joists. If the opening runs perpendicular to the floor joists, a lumber header or I-joist header made from several joists with solid wood blocking can be used. The size of each depends upon the span and any loads placed on

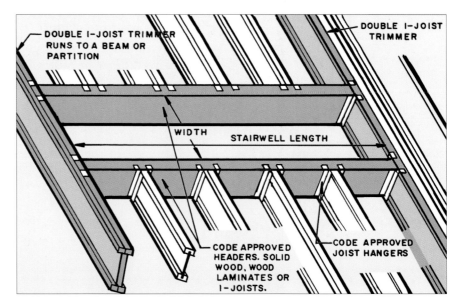

3-12 One way to frame a straight stairwell when the floor is framed with I-joists. Follow the manufacturer's instructions for assembling the I-joist and the code-approved metal joist hangers.

it from above. All connections are made with top-flange metal hangers.

Stringers are connected to the I-joist header by first installing backer blocks and filler blocks, as shown in **3-14**.

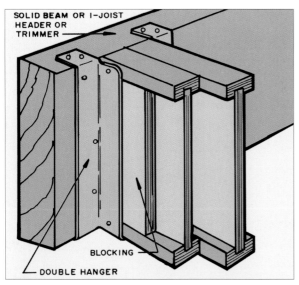

3-13 Typical construction detail for framing a stairwell when the floor is framed with I-joists.

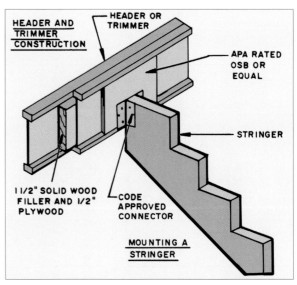

3-14 Construction detail for installing a stringer when the floor is framed with I-joists.

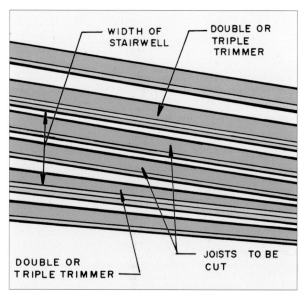

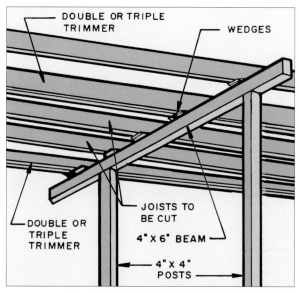

3-15 Install the trimmer joists forming the sides of the stairwell opening. They may be doubled or tripled, depending upon the load they have to carry.

3-16 Shore up the floor below the joists on each end of the stairwell opening. This holds the joists in place as the trimmers and headers are installed.

ADDING A STAIR TO AN EXISTING HOUSE

This is an ambitious project and you should first study the material in the chapters leading up to this discussion. Design the stair as discussed in Chapter 2. Once this is accomplished you must lay out and build the stairwell. Framing the stairwell is covered in this chapter.

If the existing finish floor in the room is to be replaced, remove it. If you want to save it you will need to mark the rough opening on it. You can mark it by snapping a chalkline. Then drill a hole in each corner. The holes will show from below so you can see which floor joists must be cut.

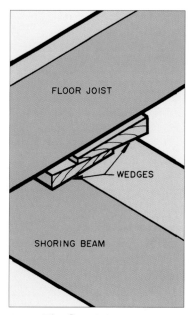

3-17 The floor joists are set firmly against the shoring beam with wood wedges.

At this point you can install the trimmers. While double trimmers will be satisfactory, some add a third trimmer to provide a margin of safety. This is especially important if there is a partition or other unusual load bearing upon the trimmers (3-15). Nail the trimmers as shown in 3-6 and hang with joist hangers as shown in 3-7.

Now you must shore up the floor joists to be cut out. Extend the shoring several joists beyond the proposed opening on each side (3-16). Drive wood wedges between the shoring and each joist so they are firmly supported by the shoring (3-17). The top plate can be toenailed to help hold it in place. Install this support at each end of the proposed opening.

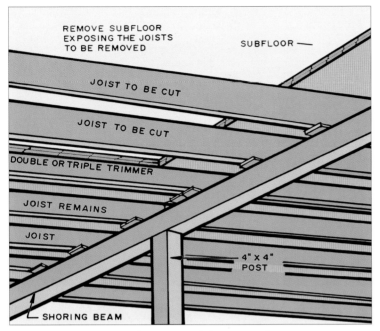

3-18 After cutting the floor around the stairwell opening, remove the finished floor and the subfloor. You can now cut the floor joists within the stairwell opening.

Consider installing a partition below each trimmer to give additional support to the floor above once the temporary shoring has been removed. Notice the use of partitions shown in **3-9** and **3-10**.

Cut through the subfloor with a portable circular saw. Set the blade deep enough to go through the subfloor about ¼ inch. Watch for nails. If one is in the path of the saw, chisel away the wood around it and pull it with a claw hammer or crow bar.

If there is solid wood flooring, it will be cut and removed first. Then saw through the subfloor and pry up the pieces, leaving the opening (**3-18**). You can drive up the subflooring from below if it is hard to pry up from above.

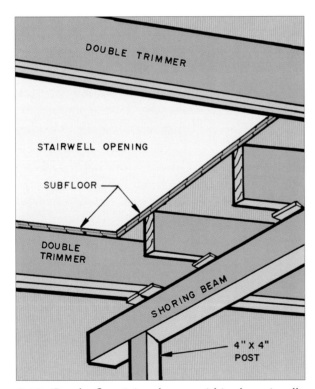

3-19 Cut the floor joists that are within the stairwell opening.

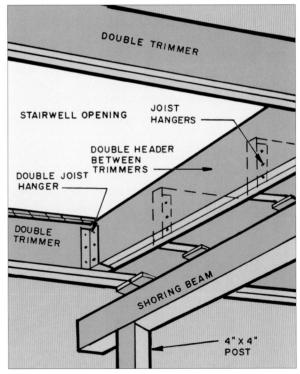

3-20 Install the header, connecting it to the trimmers and the ends of the floor joists with metal joist hangers.

3-21 A completed stairwell for a straight stair. Construction of partitions below the trimmers will provide you with a closed stairway.

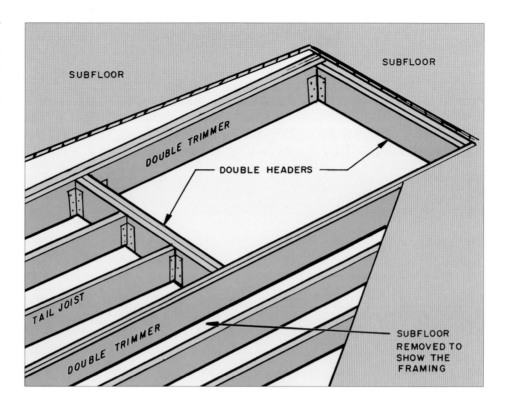

Now carefully mark and cut the joists that extend across the opening. Probably it will be easiest to cut with a fine-tooth handsaw. This leaves the opening ready for installation of the headers (**3-19**).

Add a trimmer joist to an existing joist if one is to be used or install new double or triple trimmer joists along each side of the opening. Each end should rest on the same support as the other joists as shown earlier in **3-9**.

Install the headers across the ends of the cut floor joists. The easiest way is to use double metal joist hangers to connect the header to the trimmer joists. Then connect the cut floor joists to the header with single metal joist hangers (**3-20**). You can use solid wood members or I-joists, as described earlier in this chapter. A completed stairwell is shown in **3-21**.

Now you are ready to design the stringer as described in Chapter 2. Also see the construction of a straight stair in Chapter 4. While L-shaped and U-shaped stairwells and stairs are more difficult to build, you can find this information in Chapter 5.

Straight Stairs
with Notched Stringers

The construction of a straight stair is the least complex of all types. It has no landing or turns and is a straightforward solution to providing access from one floor to another (4-1).

4-1 A straight stair provides direct access to the floor above. This stair has an open balustrade. Notice the handrail on the wall.

Courtesy Designed Stairs, Inc. 1-877-4Stairs

The following discussion relates to constructing a notched-stringer stair. The architect should have designed the stair with enough room and an adequate stairwell to allow you to build a stair that meets the code. Before you begin marking and cutting, measure the existing stairwell size and the total rise and calculate the unit rise and unit run that you will use to build the stair. It may match the sizes on the drawing. Remember that you must build a stair that meets the code or the house will not pass inspection.

STRINGER REQUIREMENTS

We will use the stair shown by the drawing in 4-2 to figure our stringer layout. The first thing to do is find out how long a piece of stock you need. You can find this by figuring the length of the hypotenuse of a triangle with sides equal to the total rise and total run. The length of the hypotenuse of a right triangle is found using the Pythagorean theorem (4-2). The use of this theorem indicates the stringer is 16.4 feet long. Since lumber is sold by 2 feet increments and you need some extra in case you need to cut some checked ends away, purchase 18 feet of long stock.

Wood for stringers must be strong, straight, and free of warp, cup, and free of all but the tiniest knots. It should be kiln dried. You should go to the lumberyard and hand-pick the pieces you want to use. Keep them dry during construction and lay them flat when stored.

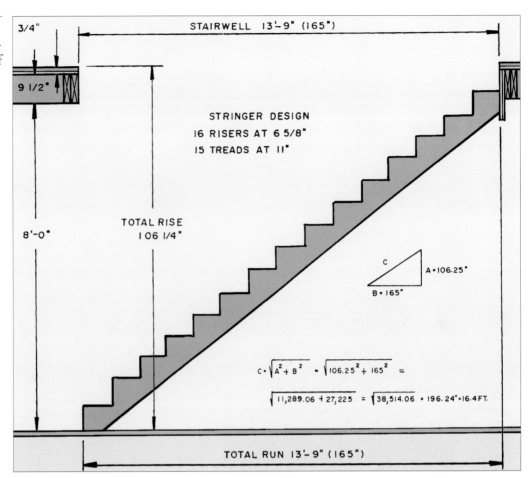

4-2 You can get the approximate length of the stringer by using the Pythagorean theorem.

STAIRWELL 13'-9" (165")

3/4"

9 1/2"

STRINGER DESIGN
16 RISERS AT 6 5/8"
15 TREADS AT 11"

TOTAL RISE
106 1/4"

8'-0"

C

A = 106.25"

B = 165"

$$C = \sqrt{A^2 + B^2} = \sqrt{106.25^2 + 165^2} =$$

$$\sqrt{11,289.06 + 27,225} = \sqrt{38,514.06} = 196.24" = 16.4 \text{ FT.}$$

TOTAL RUN 13'-9" (165")

The stringer should be wide enough to have the rise and run cut out and leave a minimum of 3-inch solid stock (4-3). Usually 2 × 12 stock is used. Interior stairs use any high-quality softwood or hardwood such as Douglas fir, hemlock, spruce, yellow pine, red fir, and white oak.

The number of stringers is determined by the width of the stair, the thickness of the treads, and the length of the stringer. Building codes specify the number required. Typically if the outer stringers are more than 30 inches apart and the tread is 1¹⁄₁₆ inch thick or if the outer stringers are 36 inches apart and the tread is 1½ inch thick, a third stringer in the center of the stair is required. Even if the code will let you use two stringers a third will stiffen and strengthen the stair and should be considered.

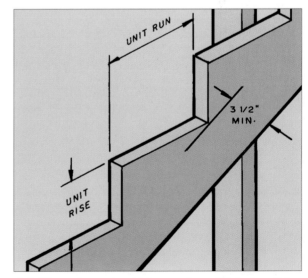

UNIT RUN

3 1/2" MIN.

UNIT RISE

4-3 The stringer should have at least 3½-inch solid stock remaining after the unit rise and unit run cuts have been made.

STRAIGHT STAIRS WITH NOTCHED STRINGERS

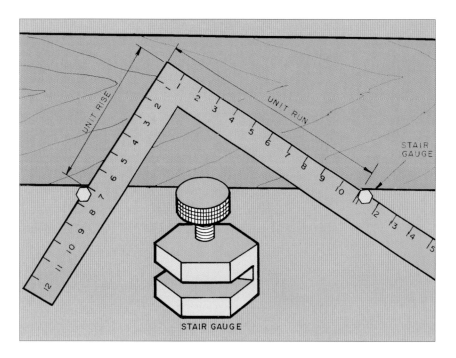

4-4 Stair gauges are used on a framing square to position it as you mark the unit rise and unit run lines.

STAIR GAUGE

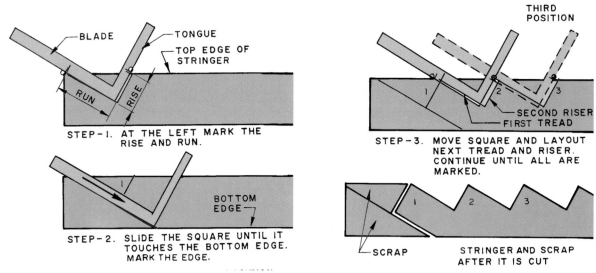

4-5 The steps to lay out the stringer using a framing square and stair gauges.

BLADE — TONGUE
TOP EDGE OF STRINGER
RUN   RISE

STEP-1. AT THE LEFT MARK THE RISE AND RUN.

BOTTOM EDGE

STEP-2. SLIDE THE SQUARE UNTIL IT TOUCHES THE BOTTOM EDGE. MARK THE EDGE.

THIRD POSITION

SECOND RISER
FIRST TREAD

STEP-3. MOVE SQUARE AND LAYOUT NEXT TREAD AND RISER. CONTINUE UNTIL ALL ARE MARKED.

SCRAP

STRINGER AND SCRAP AFTER IT IS CUT

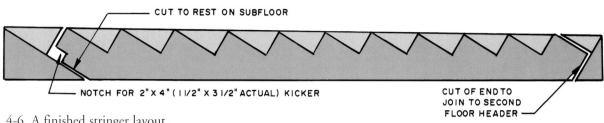

CUT TO REST ON SUBFLOOR

NOTCH FOR 2" X 4" (1 1/2" X 3 1/2" ACTUAL) KICKER

CUT OF END TO JOIN TO SECOND FLOOR HEADER

4-6 A finished stringer layout.

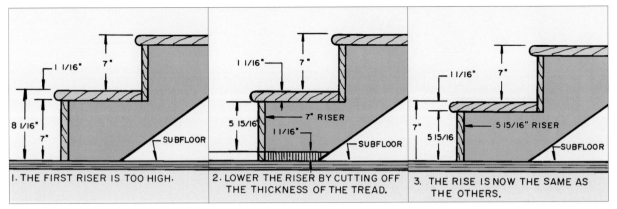

| 1. THE FIRST RISER IS TOO HIGH. | 2. LOWER THE RISER BY CUTTING OFF THE THICKNESS OF THE TREAD. | 3. THE RISE IS NOW THE SAME AS THE OTHERS. |

4-7 When the stringer is installed between floors where both levels will be carpeted over the subfloor, you have to drop the stringer a distance equal to the tread thickness.

LAYING OUT THE STRINGER

One way to lay out the stringer is to use a framing square. Clamp stair gauges on the square at the tread, and riser sizes on the blade and tongue (4-4). Stair gauges are small clamps that are fastened to the framing square. At the lower end of the 2 × 2 stock mark the bottom cut (4-5). Then move the square and mark the next riser. Continue until all tread and riser cuts have been marked. Mark them with a utility knife or a very sharp pencil. At the top of the stringer mark the plumb cut, producing the surface that butts the header at the second floor. Now lay out the notch at the floor end for the 2 × 4 kicker. A finished stringer layout is shown in 4-6.

DROPPING THE STRINGER
It is important that all risers on a stair be the same size. If they vary, this will likely cause someone to fall.

4-8 When the stringer rests on the subfloor and later solid wood flooring will be installed-drop the stringer an amount equal to the tread thickness minus the finished wood floor thickness.

Before cutting the bottom end of the stringer, check to see if it needs to be lowered to allow for conditions related to the finished floor. This is reviewed in Chapter 2 and explained in the following paragraphs.

Several situations can occur. If the subfloor on both levels is to be covered with carpet or the stringer will be placed on top of the finished flooring, as solid wood, you need to drop the stringer the thickness of one tread so the lower riser is the same as the others (4-7).

If you rest the stringer on the subfloor and will later install solid wood flooring, the thickness of the flooring will help equalize the riser height at the floor. You still must cut off the bottom of the stringer, but it will be the difference between the thickness of the tread and the solid wood flooring (4-8).

Check the design and flooring requirements for other situations that may cause the lower or upper rise distance to vary. Adjust the length of the stringer to regulate these.

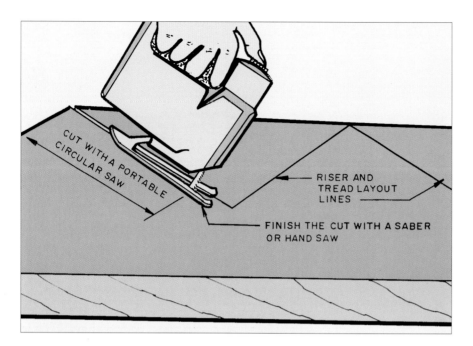

4-9 You can cut the treads and risers on the stringer with a portable circular saw, but since it undercuts, stop before you reach the end of the line and finish the cut with a saber saw or handsaw.

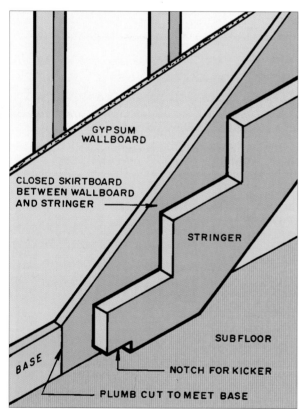

4-10 The closed skirtboard is installed between the gypsum wallboard and the stringer. It is often installed after the stringer is in place, so you must remember to leave space for it when you install the stringer.

CUTTING
THE STRINGER

The cuts are usually made with a portable circular saw. Cut very accurately, just trimming the marked line. Since the saw undercuts, you cannot cut all the way to the corner. Finish the cut with a handsaw or saber saw (4-9). After you cut one stringer, place it in the stairwell to see if it fits and if the treads are level. Then use it to mark and cut the others.

BEFORE YOU INSTALL
THE STRINGERS

Following are some things you must know before installing the stringers. If they fit against a wall and the drywall has not been installed, leave space for it to be put behind the stringer. Usually ½-inch-thick gypsum wallboard is used. Leave about ¾ inch, so there is some extra space allowed.

If the stair is to have a closed **skirtboard** it is placed between the drywall and the stringer (4-10). This is usually ¾-inch-thick wood, so this plus the drywall will require a space of about 1½ inches. If a thicker wall finish material is to be used, increase this space.

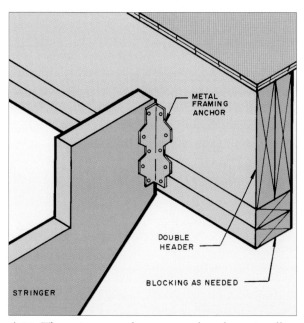

4-11 The stringer can be connected to the stairwell header with metal framing anchors.

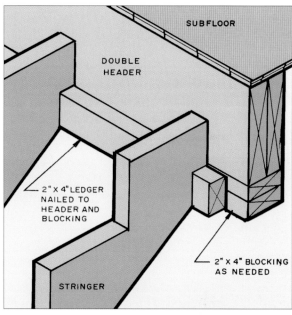

4-13 A ledger can be used to support the top of the stringer, which is then nailed to the header.

INSTALLING THE STRINGERS

There are several ways to support the top of the stringer. One way is to add blocking below the stairwell header and secure the stringer with metal hangers (4-11). Another way is to nail a ¾ inch plywood hangerboard over the header (4-12). You can usually nail or screw the stringer to the hangerboard from behind, but the addition of metal hangers provides additional support. Another method uses a ledger securely nailed to the header and the studs, as shown in 4-13.

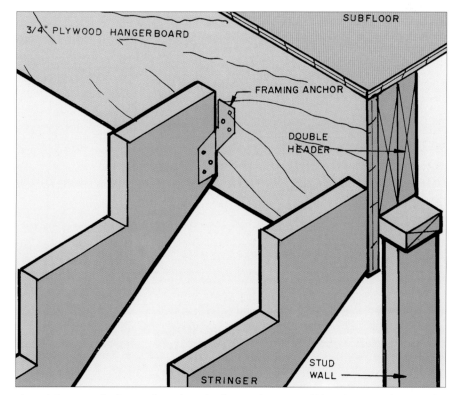

4-12 The use of a hangerboard applied over the stairwell header provides a wide and solid means for connecting the stringers at the top of the stair. The use of framing anchors strengthens the connection.

STRAIGHT STAIRS WITH NOTCHED STRINGERS

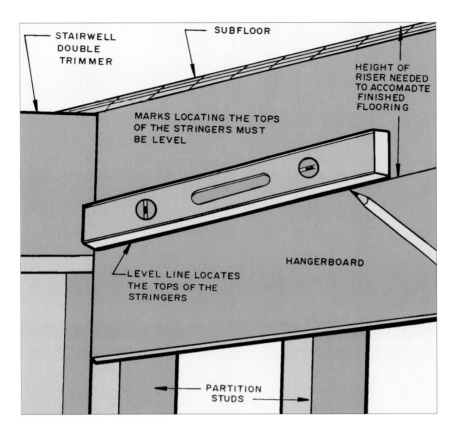

STAIRWELL DOUBLE TRIMMER

SUBFLOOR

HEIGHT OF RISER NEEDED TO ACCOMADTE FINISHED FLOORING

MARKS LOCATING THE TOPS OF THE STRINGERS MUST BE LEVEL

HANGERBOARD

LEVEL LINE LOCATES THE TOPS OF THE STRINGERS

PARTITION STUDS

4-14 Check the marks locating the tops of the stringers with a carpenter's level to be certain the treads will be level when the stair is built.

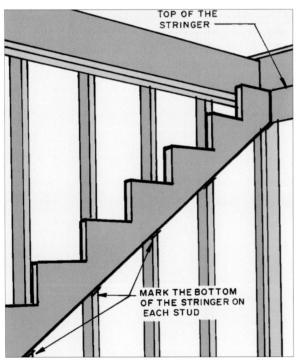

TOP OF THE STRINGER

MARK THE BOTTOM OF THE STRINGER ON EACH STUD

4-15 Temporarily place the first stringer against the studs and mark the bottom edge on each stud.

NAIL 2 X 4 BLOCKING TO THE STUDS. LINE UP WITH THE MARKS.

4-16 Remove the stringer and nail a 2 × 4 along the studs, lining up the bottom edge with the stringer marks. This provides a spacer for the gypsum wallboard and skirtboard. The stringer is nailed to this blocking and into the studs.

4-17 The stringer is nailed to the 2 × 4 blocking before the wallboard and skirtboard are in place.

4-18 This view is from behind the stringers, showing 2 × 4 blocking nailed to the center stringer.

Begin by marking the location of the top of the stringer on the header or hangerboard (4-14). Check to be certain it is level. Temporarily place the stringer next to a wall first and tack it to the hangerboard. Mark the bottom edge on each stud (4-15). Then nail 2 × 4 blocking to the stud, lining the bottom up with the mark (4-16). This provides a solid nailing surface to which the stringer will be nailed, and spaces it out from the studs, allowing space for the gypsum wallboard and skirtboard (4-17).

The center stringer has 2 × 4 blocking nailed on each side. This stiffens it and provides a nailing surface if gypsum wallboard is to cover the bottom of the stair (4-18).

Install the other outside stringer. Check to see that the treads are level. Then install the center stringer (4-19).

Position the bottom end of the first stringer against the blocking on the studs. Set the kickboard in place and position the stringers on the kickboard. If they are all an equal distance apart and level, toenail to the kickboard. You can check the kickboard to see if the lower tread will be level. If not, shim it as needed to get it level (4-19). The kickboard should not extend beyond the side of the stringer. If it does, it will be in the way of the skirtboard and drywall. When all is set, finish connecting the top of the stringers to the hangerboard. Then nail through the side stringer into the blocking on the wall.

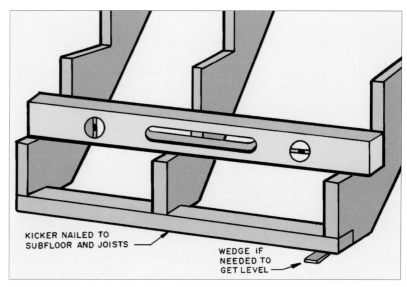

KICKER NAILED TO
SUBFLOOR AND JOISTS

WEDGE IF
NEEDED TO
GET LEVEL

4-19 As you install the stringers, check that the tread cuts are level.

STRAIGHT STAIRS WITH NOTCHED STRINGERS

43

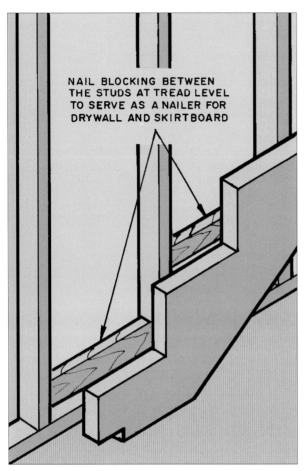

NAIL BLOCKING BETWEEN THE STUDS AT TREAD LEVEL TO SERVE AS A NAILER FOR DRYWALL AND SKIRTBOARD

4-20 Two-inch-thick blocking is nailed between the wall studs at the tread level so you can nail the gypsum wallboard and skirtboard to the wall.

4-21 Temporary 2 × 4 treads are installed to give the workers access to the second floor. Notice the mess on them from taping the gypsum wallboard.

After the stringers are in place, nail some 2 × 6 blocking at the tread level to provide a nailer for the drywall and skirtboard (4-20).

In 4-21 notice that temporary 2 × 4 boards have been nailed as treads. This provides temporary access to the next level. The stair will be finished after all the other trades have completed their work.

If you have a stair that has one stringer exposed, you can stiffen it by building a stud wall below, as shown in 4-22. This also can provide a storage area. You can also double this stringer or nail a 2 × 4 piece along the bottom edge to stiffen it.

The exposed stringer may be covered with an exposed notched skirtboard to provide an attractive appearance. Typically it is covered with gypsum drywall or a decorative wood (4-23).

CUTTING & INSTALLING THE SKIRTBOARD

The skirtboard is used to protect the wallboard along the side of the stair that butts a wall. It is also a decorative feature (4-24).

Some builders prefer to wait to install the stringers until after the wallboard is in place. They then set the stringers and place the skirt-

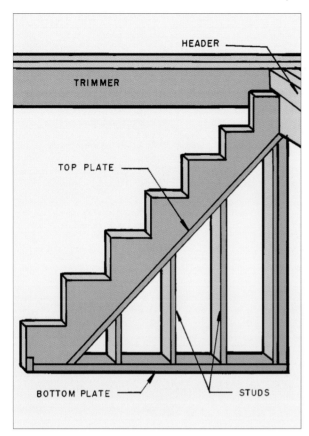

4-22 A stringer on an open stair can be stiffened by building a partition below. This also creates a storage area.

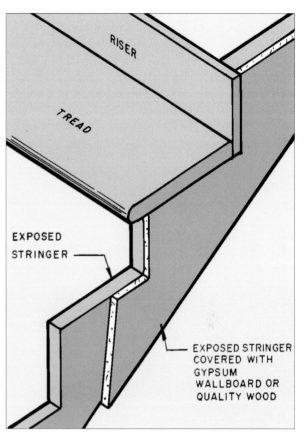

4-23 The rough exposed stringer is covered with a quality-wood notched skirtboard or gypsum wallboard.

board between the wallboard and the stringer. The stringer is set 1 inch away from the wallboard to allow the skirtboard to be slipped in place (4-21). Other builders will set the stringers before the wallboard is installed. They leave a 1½ inch space between the studs and the side of the stringer. The wallboard and skirtboard are installed at a later time.

The skirtboard is not a required part of a stair but it is used to cover the drywall at the end of the treads and to protect it from damage. Generally a clear, straight 1 × 10 board will be adequate for the skirtboard. It should extend above the nosing enough to give sufficient width to butt the baseboard on the floor. Usually one to two inches is enough.

4-24 The skirtboard protects the wall along the side of a closed stair.

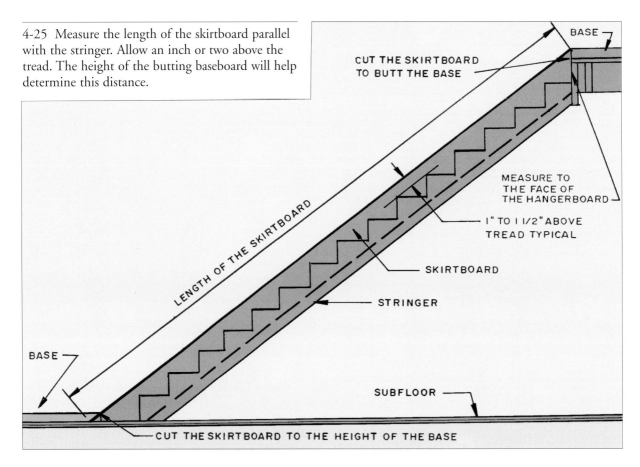

4-25 Measure the length of the skirtboard parallel with the stringer. Allow an inch or two above the tread. The height of the butting baseboard will help determine this distance.

CUT THE SKIRTBOARD TO BUTT THE BASE

BASE

MEASURE TO THE FACE OF THE HANGERBOARD

1" TO 1 1/2" ABOVE TREAD TYPICAL

SKIRTBOARD

STRINGER

LENGTH OF THE SKIRTBOARD

BASE

SUBFLOOR

CUT THE SKIRTBOARD TO THE HEIGHT OF THE BASE

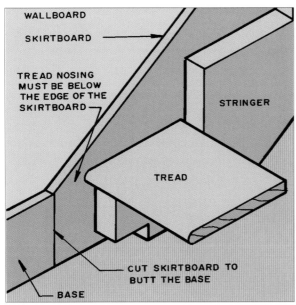

WALLBOARD

SKIRTBOARD

TREAD NOSING MUST BE BELOW THE EDGE OF THE SKIRTBOARD

STRINGER

TREAD

CUT SKIRTBOARD TO BUTT THE BASE

BASE

4-26 Check to be certain that the skirtboard is high enough to allow the tread nosing to clear the top edge. The amount of space left is a design decision.

To lay out the skirt, measure the length from the top of the stair at the riser to the floor below. Run the tape parallel with the nosing and an inch or so above it, as you wish (4-25). Check at the floor to be certain the skirtboard clears the nosing enough on the last tread board so the baseboard on the wall can neatly butt the skirt (4-26).

When the skirtboard meets the second floor or a landing that is to be carpeted, the plywood subfloor is extended forming a nosing. Notch this nosing to allow the end of the skirtboard to butt the hangerboard, as shown in 4-27. If there is to be a solid wood finished flooring it will have a nosing made from the flooring. The nosing will be notched to receive the skirtboard, the same as the plywood subfloor (4-28). The skirtboard is nailed to the blocking placed between the studs, as shown in 4-20.

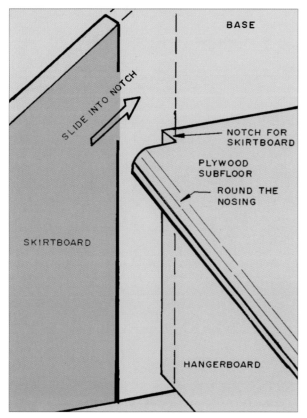

4-27 Notch the plywood subfloor to receive the skirtboard when the finish floor will be carpet.

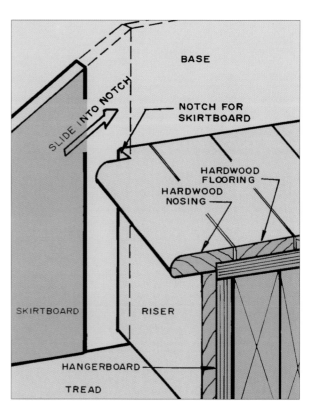

4-28 When the finish floor will be solid wood notch the nosing strip to receive the skirtboard.

If the stringer is placed against the gypsum wallboard, you can install a notched skirtboard as shown in 4-29. This only leaves about   inch of bearing surface on the stringer for the treads and risers.

The exposed edge of the skirtboard may be left square, have a molding nailed above it, or be shaped with a router (4-30).

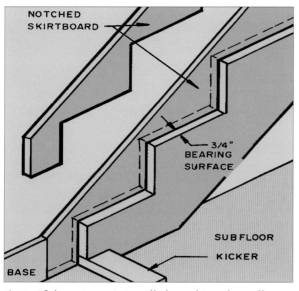

4-29 If the stringer is installed touching the wall-board, a notched skirtboard can be used to provide protection.

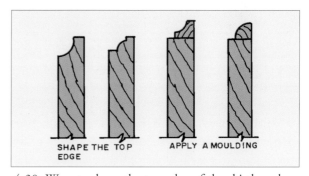

4-30 Ways to shape the top edge of the skirtboard.

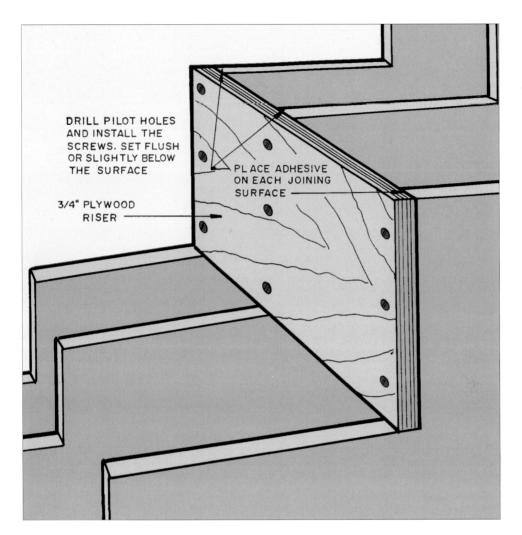

DRILL PILOT HOLES
AND INSTALL THE
SCREWS. SET FLUSH
OR SLIGHTLY BELOW
THE SURFACE

PLACE ADHESIVE
ON EACH JOINING
SURFACE

3/4" PLYWOOD
RISER

4-31 Secure the plywood riser to the stringer with adhesive and screws. Be certain the heads are flush or a little below the surface.

INSTALLING TREADS & RISERS FOR CARPETED STAIRS USING NOTCHED STRINGERS

Treads and risers for stairs to be covered with carpet are often cut from ¾-inch plywood. It is even better to use 1⅛-inch plywood for the treads. You must decide which is to be used before you plan the stair, because it will influence the design of the stringer.

The sequence for installing risers and treads varies. Some install the bottom and top risers first and then install a couple in the center of the stair. This will help hold the stringers in line as you install those remaining.

Install the risers by coating the bonding surface on the stringer with adhesive. Place the riser against this and drill pilot holes through it and secure with 2-inch drywall screws. Use at least two screws into each stringer surface. The glue helps reduce the possibility of squeaks occurring (4-31).

The treads are installed much the same way. Apply adhesive to the stringer and the top edge of the riser and the back edge of the tread. Place the tread firmly against the riser and secure to the stringer with at least three 2-inch drywall screws. Drill pilot holes for the screws and be certain the heads are flush or just below the surface of the plywood (4-32).

4-32 Secure the plywood tread to the stringer with adhesive and screws. The back edge is coated with adhesive and screwed to the riser.

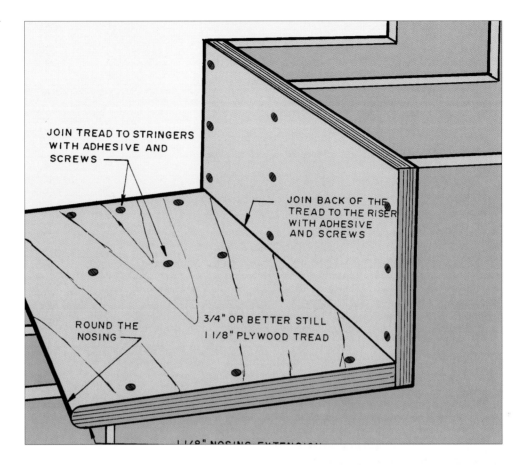

JOIN TREAD TO STRINGERS WITH ADHESIVE AND SCREWS

JOIN BACK OF THE TREAD TO THE RISER WITH ADHESIVE AND SCREWS

ROUND THE NOSING

3/4" OR BETTER STILL 1 1/8" PLYWOOD TREAD

1 1/8" NOSING EXTENSION

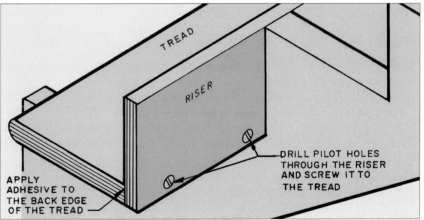

4-33 Glue and screw the riser to the back of the tread.

TREAD

RISER

APPLY ADHESIVE TO THE BACK EDGE OF THE TREAD

DRILL PILOT HOLES THROUGH THE RISER AND SCREW IT TO THE TREAD

Finally, drill pilot holes through the bottom of the riser and drive several screws into the edge of the tread. This stiffens the assembly and reduces the possibility of squeaks (**4-33**). Slightly countersink the screw holes if necessary, to keep the head flush or slightly below the surface of the tread.

The front edge of the plywood tread should be rounded so that the carpet will wrap smoothly around it. These front edges of each tread should extend 1⅛ inch beyond the riser. At the second floor prepare the nosing as shown in 4-27 on page 47.

4-34 Quality construction will join treads and risers with tongue-and-groove joints, glue, screws, and glue blocks.

4-36 This type of construction uses butt joints, nails, and glue. It will eventually lead to squeaks.

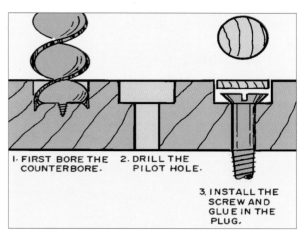

1. FIRST BORE THE COUNTERBORE. 2. DRILL THE PILOT HOLE.

3. INSTALL THE SCREW AND GLUE IN THE PLUG.

4-35 The exposed screws on the hardwood treads are set in a counterbore and covered with a wood plug.

HARDWOOD TREADS & RISERS ON NOTCHED STRINGERS

Hardwood treads and risers are used on stairs where they will be exposed and are finished in the same manner as hardwood flooring. Stock sizes are available from stair-parts manufacturers. While oak is probably most commonly used, other quality woods, such as maple and birch, are also used. These come in standard sizes so you will have to cut them to fit your stair. Risers are typically ¾ inch thick and treads 1¹⁄₁₆ inch thick.

Typical floor, tread, and riser construction when the landing or second floor is finished with solid wood flooring is shown in **4-28**. Notice that the riser will cover the edge of the subflooring. This has to be figured in as the stair is designed.

In **4-34** is shown the best way to connect hardwood treads and risers. The treads and risers have tongue-and-groove joints, are glued, and are supported with glue blocks. They are screwed to the notched riser. The tongue-and-groove joint will help conceal any movement and possible crack occurring between the tread and riser. The screws in the tread are set in counterbored holes and wood plugs of the same wood are glued in the counterbore (**4-35** and **4-36**).

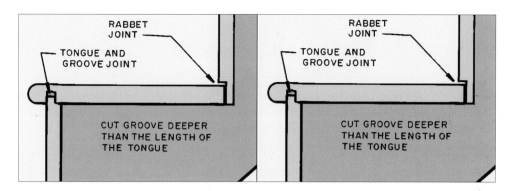

Courtesy Arcways, Inc. 1-800-558-5096

4-37 A rabbet in the end of the riser can help hide small cracks that may occur. Small moldings can also be used.

Many stairs are built with treads and risers butting, as shown in **4-36**. They are often nailed instead of joined with screws. These will eventually begin to squeak. Glue blocks would strengthen this installation.

Sometimes a small molding is nailed over the crack between the tread and riser. Nail it with wire brads to the riser so the tread can slide back and forth under it. Another technique is to cut a rabbet in the bottom edge of the riser. Either of these will help conceal the crack between the tread and riser (**4-37**).

In all cases install glue blocks between the treads and risers from behind the stair. This will help reduce squeaks. Install two to four blocks in a 36-inch-wide stair. Each block is typically 3 to 4 inches long (**4-34**).

Hardwood treads and risers on notched stringers will butt the skirtboard on a closed stair. This will require that the ends of the treads and risers be cleanly cut to produce the least visible joint. If this is objectionable, you should use a housed stringer.

The installation of the treads and risers can be handled several ways. They can be installed with the end grain exposed to view, as shown in **4-38**. Treads having a radiused return covering the end grain provide a more attractive solution (**4-39**).

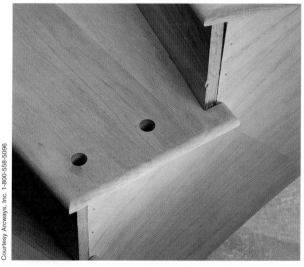

Courtesy Arcways, Inc. 1-800-558-5096

4-38 This stair has the edge of the trend machined round but shows the coarse end grain. The end of the riser is also exposing end grain. If the fit is poor (as shown) a crack will appear.

Courtesy Arcways, Inc. 1-800-558-5096

4-39 This high-quality tread and riser construction shows the radiused return on the edge of the tread providing attractive side grain. The riser and skirtboard are mitered forming a good-looking closed corner.

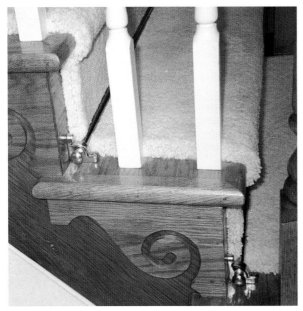

4-40 The end grain of an exposed square-end riser can be concealed by installing ¼-inch-thick stair brackets.

Appearance is improved by mitering the riser and the adjoining exposed skirtboard, as shown in **4-39** on the previous page. (Construction details are shown in **4-42**.)

Instead of mitering the skirtboard, you could install a stair bracket that may or may not be mitered. If it is not mitered, only a ¼ inch edge grain is seen (**4-40**).

Remember that when installing an exposed skirt it should be about ⅟₁₆ inch below the bottom of the tread. In this way all the weight on the treads goes to the stringer and there is none on the skirt. If the skirt is under load, it will most likely fail. This crack is covered with molding (**4-41**). This molding extends across the front of the stair, covering any crack that may open between the bottom of the tread and the top of the riser.

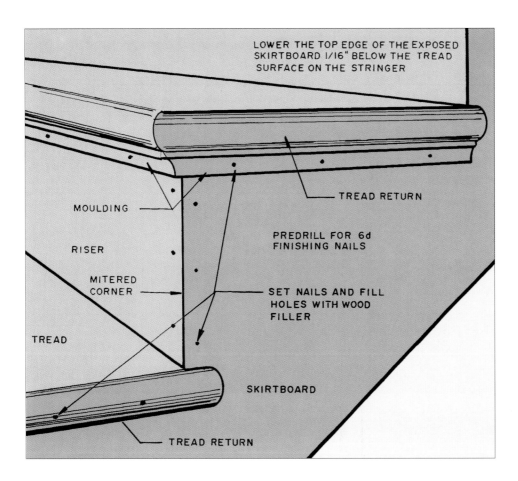

LOWER THE TOP EDGE OF THE EXPOSED
SKIRTBOARD 1/16" BELOW THE TREAD
SURFACE ON THE STRINGER

TREAD RETURN

MOULDING

RISER

PREDRILL FOR 6d
FINISHING NAILS

MITERED
CORNER

SET NAILS AND FILL
HOLES WITH WOOD
FILLER

TREAD

SKIRTBOARD

TREAD RETURN

4-41 The crack between the tread and the skirtboard on the exposed side can be covered with a small molding.

HOW TO MITER THE SKIRTBOARD OR RISER

A finished skirtboard and riser are shown in **4-39** and **4-41**. Typical details of the mitered riser–skirtboard construction are shown in **4-42**.

To lay out a mitered skirtboard:

Lay out the treads and risers on the skirtboards, as discussed for notched risers.

If the riser and skirtboard are the same thickness, draw a 45-degree line from the riser line. If they are a different thickness, 45 degrees will not work. You will need to make a drawing like the one in **4-43** and measure the needed angle for the miter. Notice in **4-41** that when the skirtboard is installed on the stringer you must add the thickness of the skirtboard to the length of the riser in order to complete the miter on the riser.

If the stringer has a partition below (as shown earlier in **4-22** on page 45), then the studs and the stringer will be covered with gypsum wallboard, paneling, or other finished wall covering. In that case the skirtboard is installed over the wall covering, so the length of the riser has to be increased to cover both the wallboard and skirtboard as shown in **4-44**.

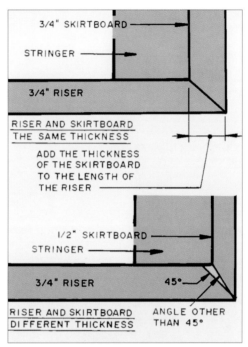

4-43 When the skirtboard is nailed directly to the stringer and they are the same thickness they are cut on a 45-degree angle. If they are different thicknesses you will have to figure the angle of the miter. This thickness is added to the length of the riser.

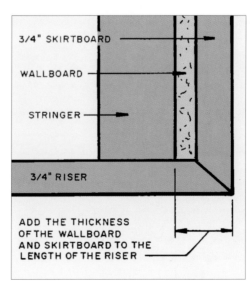

4-44 When the stringer is over a partition the thickness of the wall covering and the thickness of the skirtboard must be added to the length of the riser.

4-42 Mitering the riser and skirtboard.

As you mark the miter notice that it must slope away from the face of the skirtboard. Remember that there are right-hand and left-hand skirts, so get the miter angle heading toward the inside face of the skirtboard, as shown in **4-45**.

Some builders cut the miter slightly less than 45 degrees. This produces a tight joint at the exposed corner. The joint is open slightly at the back, but the entire thing is covered by the tread (**4-46**).

When you install the riser, check the miter for fit. The easiest way to close it is to plane a little off the heel. You could also trim the heel on the circular saw or radial arm saw. All you need to do is cut off a bit of sawdust.

Now apply adhesive to both parts of the miter and nail with 6d finish nails. It is best to predrill the holes so you do not split the miter. Nail from both sides of the joint. Set the heads so the painter can cover them with the proper color wood filler. Refer back to **4-41**.

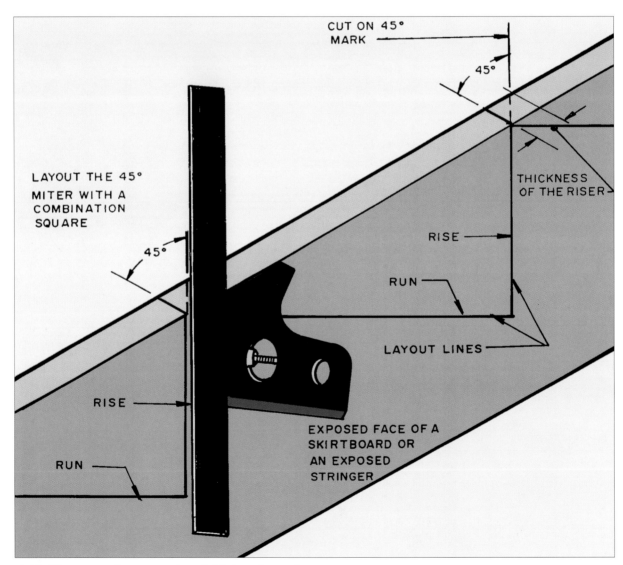

4-45 The steps to lay out a mitered skirtboard or stringer.

HOW TO MITER
THE STRINGERS

If the exposed stringer on an open stair is cut from quality hardwood or softwood, it may be left exposed and finished without needing a skirtboard. To improve the riser-stringer corner miter the stringer and riser. To do this:

1. Lay out the stringer as described earlier. Then mark the miter from the front corner of the riser line. This is the same as shown for mitered skirtboard in **4-45**.

2. Cut on the miter line.

3. Miter the skirtboard.

4. Install by gluing and nailing with 6d finishing nails, as shown in **4-41** on page 52. The finished assembly will appear as shown in **4-47**.

You can cover the end grain on the tread by making a mitered return (**4-48**).

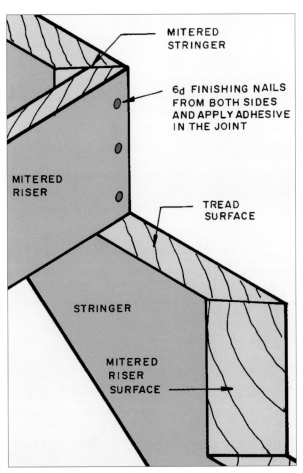

4-47 Mitering the stringer and riser.

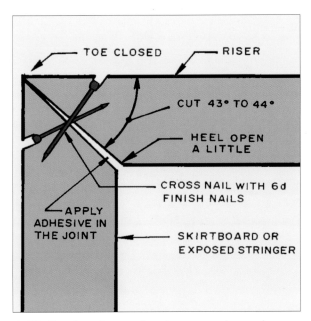

4-46 Cut the miter so that the toe touches and a small gap occurs at the heel.

4-48 A mitered return on the tread covers the rough end grain and provides a pleasing appearance.

Covering the end grain of the tread with a mitered return is difficult to make and requires careful layout and cutting. Sharp, fine-toothed saws are necessary to get a smooth cut and not chip the edges. Make the cuts required before cutting the tread to length so that if you make a mistake you might be able to salvage the tread (4-49).

You must cut the return piece just as carefully. It can often be cut from pieces of tread cut off as the tread board is cut to width. Check each one against a tread to be certain it is a tight fit.

You can make the straight cut with a table saw or radial-arm saw, but stop before you reach the actual miter. Finish cutting the miter with a fine-toothed handsaw.

Stair parts manufacturers will supply the treads with the return already installed.

The back end of the tread return sticks over the skirtboard a distance equal to the width of the return and is machined round, giving a neat finished appearance (4-50), or you can miter the return and install a piece of the return as shown in 4-51.

An easy way to handle the end return is to buy the stair treads with the return already in place. The return is extended beyond the back of the tread so you can cut it to length as desired.

STARTING STEPS

Starting steps are available with single left- and right-side and double bullnoses (4-52). Some companies manufacture a bow front unit. The manufacturer also supplies straight and curved molding to trim the step at the floor and below the tread.

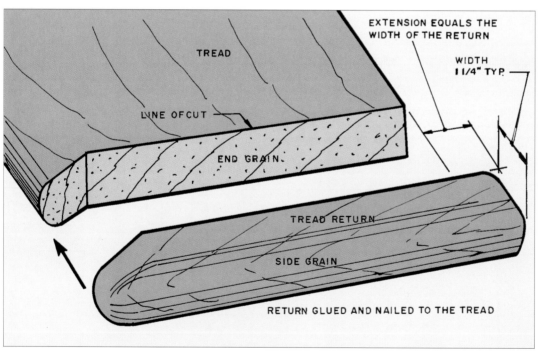

4-49 The nosing forming the mitered return is glued and nailed to the tread. It is often cut from leftover pieces of treads. The nosing exposes side grain having the appearance of the end of the tread.

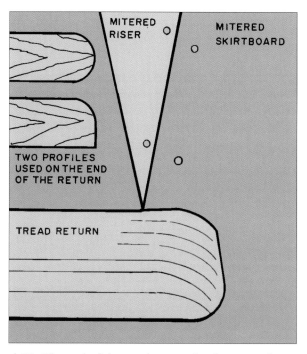

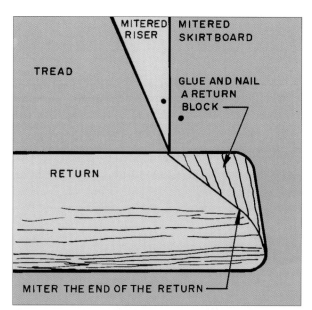

4-50 The end of the tread return that laps over the skirtboard can be finished in several ways.

4-51 One way to finish the end of the tread return is to return it by mitering the end and then inserting a mitered block. Drill a hole through the piece so the nail does not split the block. Bond with adhesive as well as the nail.

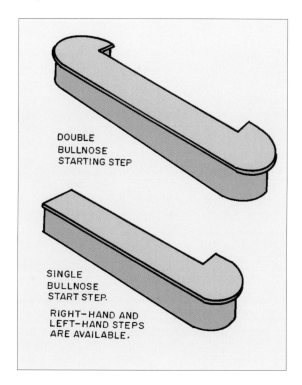

4-52 Starting steps add to the appearance of the stairway.

HOW TO INSTALL
THE STARTING STEP

Following is a typical installation procedure. Place adhesive on the stringer risers, the top and bottom edge of the starting step riser, and the side of the stringer where the bullnose riser will press against it (4-53). Place the step in place against the stringer risers. Drill small pilot holes through the starting step riser and nail to the stringer with finishing nails. Set the heads so they can be covered when the stair is finished. Drive a couple of finishing nails through the side of the bullnose that butts the side of the stringer (4-53). The stringer riser is a little higher than the height of the bullnose riser. This lets the tread bear fully on the stringer an puts no pressure on the bullnose riser.

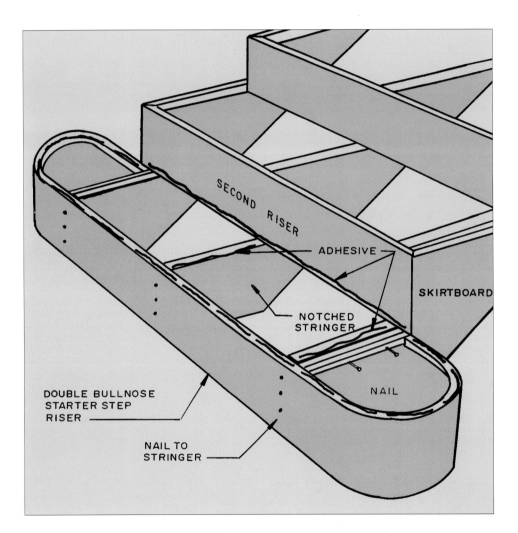

4-53 Connect the curved riser to the stringer and the floor with adhesive and finishing nails.

4-54 Bond the tread to the stringer and curved riser with adhesive and finishing nails. Secure to the second riser with screws from behind the second riser.

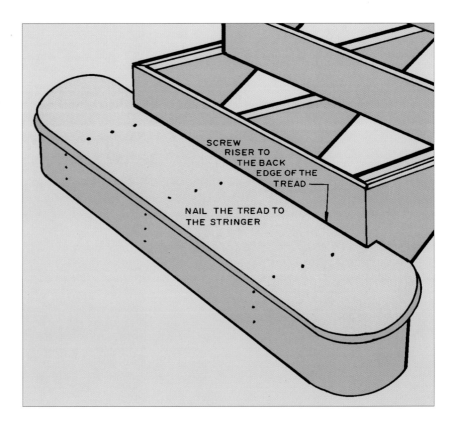

SCREW
RISER TO
THE BACK
EDGE OF THE
TREAD

NAIL THE TREAD TO
THE STRINGER

Now place adhesive on the tread-bearing surfaces of the stringer and on the bottom edge of the riser on the second step. Place the tread on the riser and then nail with finishing nails. Set the nails. Finally, join the second riser to the starting step tread with several screws through the riser into the back of the tread (4-54).

Now install the curved and straight cove molding below the tread and the curved and straight shoe molding where the bullnose starting step meets the floor.

The newel is bolted to the starting step, producing an attractive entrance to the stairway. A finished installation of the starting step with the balustrade newel is shown in 4-55.

4-55 The finished starting step with the balustrade newel secured to the tread.

Stairs Using Housed Stringers

A housed stringer is considered the best method for framing a stair because each tread and riser is set into a mortise cut into the side of the stringer (**5-1**). The ends of the risers and treads are hidden so tthat no crack appears. Each mortise is wider at the back than at the front. The front end of the tread mortise is machined rounded to fit the tread nosing (**5-2**).

A properly made housed tread and riser are shown in **5-3**. Notice that the curved end of the tread fits exactly into the mortise. The riser fits snuggly against the front edge of the riser mortise. If these are carelessly cut, you will have cracks as shown in **5-4**.

As the treads and risers are installed in the mortises, they are glued and bonded with a wedge driven from the back side, pressing them tightly against the exposed edges of the mortises (**5-5**).

LAYING OUT A HOUSED STRINGER

Housed stringers are made from stock 1¼ or 1½ inches thick and 11½ inches wide. Cut the mortise ⅜ inch deep. Stringers should be straight, kiln dried, and free from all defects.

Stairs with housed stringers are often bought from stair manufacturers who machine the mortises in the stringers and supply the wedges, treads, and risers.

Courtesy Designed Stairs, Inc. 1-877-4Stairs

5-1 The treads on this open stair are set into mortises cut into a housed stringer. This provides a tight, crack-free tread to stringer connection. Housed stringers are also widely used on quality stairs that have closed risers.

5-2 Housed stringers have mortises cut into them into which the treads and risers are secured.

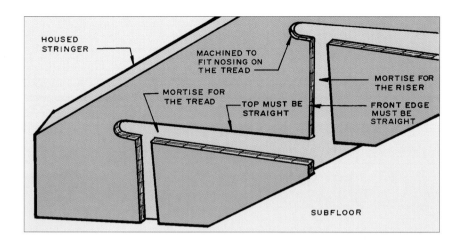

5-3 A quality housed tread and riser installation. The tread nosing fits the curved end of the mortise tightly. The surfaces of the tread and riser butt tightly against the sides of the mortise.

5-4 The mortises on this housed stringer are poorly cut. They are sized too large and are not straight, causing cracks to appear that produce an unsightly installation.

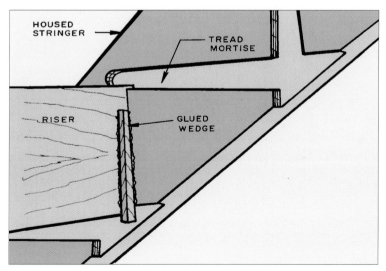

5-5 The treads and risers are held in the mortises by glued wood wedges.

5-6 Stair manufacturers frequently use housed stringers on stairs where the stringer mounts against a wall.

Courtesy The Hardwood Company 1-800-771-5006

As you begin the layout planning, remember that for a closed stair you will need to lay out and cut **right-hand** and **left-hand stringers,** or a stair open on one side you will need either a right-hand or left-hand side, depending upon which side of the stair is to be open. The open side will often use a notched stringer with the tread overhanging the skirtboard, as shown in **5-6.**

While there are several procedures used to lay out the mortises, the following is typical. The basic layout is shown in **5-7.**

1. Draw the stringer layout line ½ to 2 inches from the bottom edge. The riser and tread lines are measured along this line, rather than the edge of the stringer as is done with notched risers. This allows room for the riser and tread boards to be supported by wedges.

2. Lay out the riser and tread lines from the layout line. Remember that the tread does not include the nosing on the tread board. This is the same procedure as laying out a notched stringer.

3. Lay out the floor cut. It is parallel with the tread. In some cases (as discussed in the notched stringer section) this riser height has to be adjusted because of conditions at the floor.

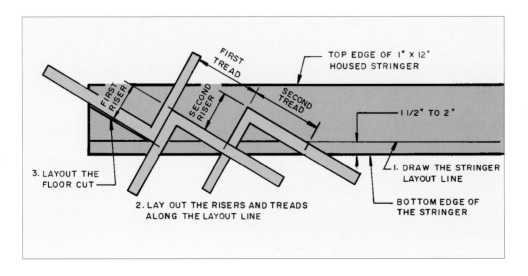

5-7 The basic steps for laying out the treads and risers for a housed stringer. These are similar to those used for the notched stringer.

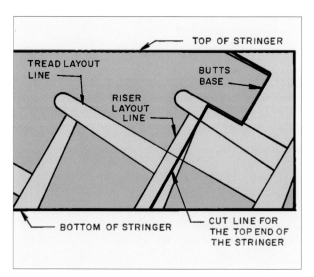

5-8 This figure shows the cut lines at the top of a housed stringer. The riser butts the header. The stringer overlaps the second floor and butts the base.

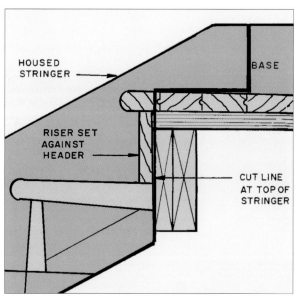

5-9 The housed stringer installed at the second level.

4. Lay out the top cut to fit around the floor at the second level as shown in **5-8.** The top riser fits against the hangerboard. The tread nosing mortise fits around the nosing board that is part of the wood floor on the second level. The installation of the housed stringer at the second level is shown in the layout in **5-9.**

5. Make templates showing the actual size of the riser and tread, plus the wedge to be used to hold them in place (**5-10**). The tread template will include the nosing. Draw the rounded nosing so it is exactly the same as on the tread to be used. You can trace around a piece of tread board to get this arc.

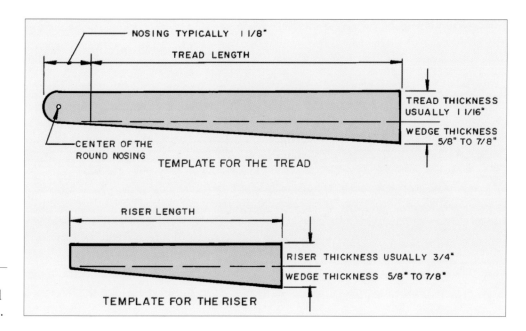

5-10 Make templates of the tread and riser mortises.

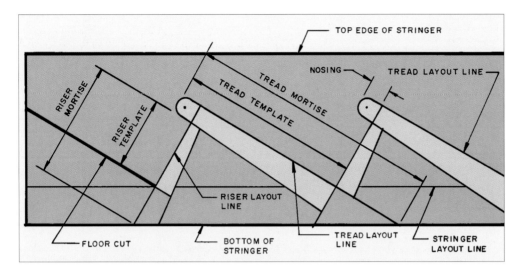

TOP EDGE OF STRINGER

NOSING — TREAD LAYOUT LINE

TREAD MORTISE

TREAD TEMPLATE

RISER MORTISE

RISER TEMPLATE

RISER LAYOUT LINE

FLOOR CUT

BOTTOM OF STRINGER

TREAD LAYOUT LINE

STRINGER LAYOUT LINE

5-11 Place the tread and riser templates on the stringer with their top edges on the layout lines. Carefully mark around the edges of the templates.

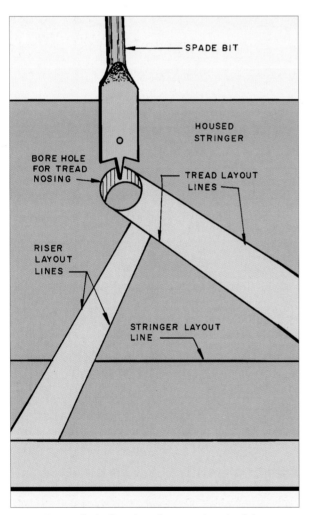

SPADE BIT

HOUSED STRINGER

BORE HOLE FOR TREAD NOSING

TREAD LAYOUT LINES

RISER LAYOUT LINES

STRINGER LAYOUT LINE

5-12 Bore a hole forming the round end of the mortise into which the tread nosing will fit.

6. Lay the templates on the stringers and mark their outlines. The riser and tread lines on the stringers are the exposed sides, so the template is placed below them. Mark the center of the nosing. This is used when boring the opening for the nosing with a spade drill. The nosing will extend one inch beyond the riser line (5-11).

CUTTING THE MORTISES

Carpenter-built housed stringers have the mortise machined with a router. The round end for the tread nosing is bored with a spade bit (5-12). The round nosing on the treads you are going to use may be a perfect circle or a segment of a larger arc (5-13). If you machine your own treads you can round the nosing with a router or shaper in a perfect circle. This way it will fit snuggly against the bored hole in the stringer. If you buy manufactured treads, check the shape of the rounded nosing. If it is a segment of a larger circle, you will have to lightly trim the bored hole to fit this slightly different arc (5-13).

The mortise is routed ⅜ inch deep. Carpenters have different ways of doing this, but many make some kind of template to guide the router base or the router cutter. Whatever is used, it is important to route the mortise very

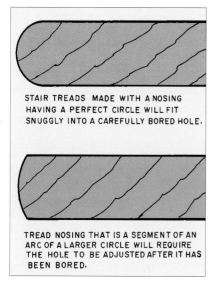

STAIR TREADS MADE WITH A NOSING HAVING A PERFECT CIRCLE WILL FIT SNUGGLY INTO A CAREFULLY BORED HOLE.

TREAD NOSING THAT IS A SEGMENT OF AN ARC OF A LARGER CIRCLE WILL REQUIRE THE HOLE TO BE ADJUSTED AFTER IT HAS BEEN BORED.

5-13 Treads with a perfectly round nosing will fit snuggly into the bored nosing hole.

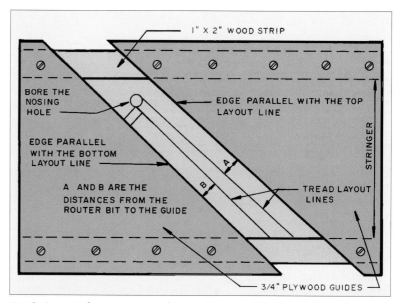

5-14 A typical carpenter-made template to guide the router as it routes the mortise on a housed stringer.

accurately. If you prefer, you could cut the edges of the mortise with a portable circular saw and route out the wood between the kerfs.

In **5-14** is a typical carpenter-built guide used to guide the router as it cuts the mortise. You will need another like it designed to cut the riser mortise. Clamp them securely to the stringer.

The router base slides along the edge of the guide, as shown in **5-15**. Some prefer to bore the nosing hole and route it as shown.

The stair builder uses a powerful plunge router to cut the mortises. It allows the bit to be lowered directly into the stringer and then moved along the guide to form the mortise (**5-16**).

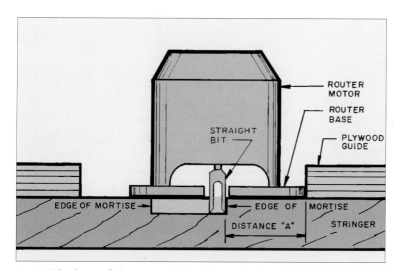

5-15 The base of the router slides along the edge of the plywood guide.

5-16 The mortise is cut with a powerful plunge router.

THE WEDGES

The size of the wedge varies. Generally the wedge is around ⅝ to ⅞ inch on the wide end. The wedge should not end in a sharp point (5-17). A blunt end is needed so that it binds before it reaches the back of the tread or riser. If it jambs against them, you will not be able to drive it enough to get the wedging force required (5-18). Cut the wedge about ½ inch shorter than

the unit rise or run. Some prefer to cut longer and trim as necessary as the stair is assembled.

If you cut your own wedges a radial arm saw or a chop saw is convenient to use. Set the blade at one-half the wedge angle. Place the stock against the fence and take a cut. Flip the stock edge for edge against the fence and take another cut (5-19). When the piece being cut becomes a bit small, discard it. Do not try to use every bit of it; this places your fingers too close to the saw blade.

Remember that each tread and riser requires two wedges, so be certain to cut enough.

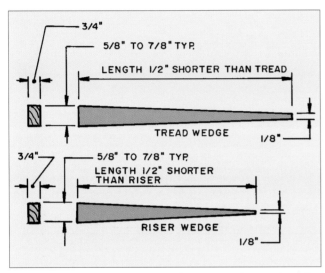

5-17 Typical wood wedges used to secure the treads and risers to housed stringers.

ASSEMBLING THE HOUSED STAIR

Many prefer to assemble housed stairs that run between two housed stringers before they are raised into the stairwell. Following are the things you need to do to complete the assembly.

1. First, ascertain the length of the treads and risers. This is critical because the assembled stair will have to fit into an already built stairwell and leave room for the drywall. Notice in **5-20** that the finished stair from outside to outside of the stringers is 36 inches, The finished opening should be about 1inch wider than the assembled stair.

2. Now examine the housed stringers. Assuming ours are 1¼ inch thick and the mortise is ⅜ inch deep, the length of the treads and risers is 36 inches minus 1¾ inches or 34¼ inches. The 1¾ inch is found by subtracting the depth of the mortise from the thickness of the stringer and doubling it, because there are two stringers (5-21).

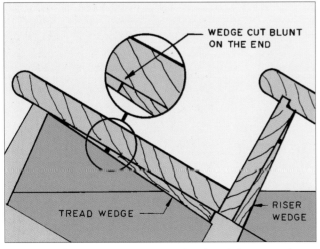

5-18 The blunt end wedges are glued and driven in the mortise behind the treads and risers.

3. Cut the treads and the risers to length and width.

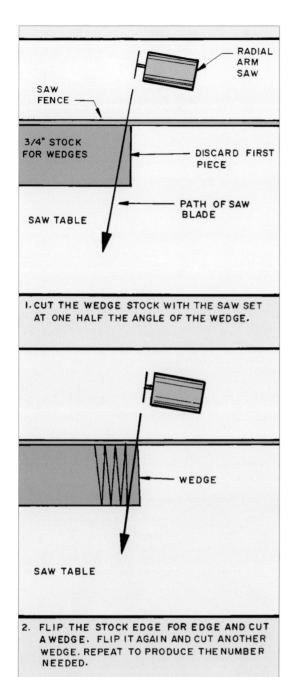

RADIAL ARM SAW

SAW FENCE

3/4" STOCK FOR WEDGES

DISCARD FIRST PIECE

SAW TABLE

PATH OF SAW BLADE

1. CUT THE WEDGE STOCK WITH THE SAW SET AT ONE HALF THE ANGLE OF THE WEDGE.

WEDGE

SAW TABLE

2. FLIP THE STOCK EDGE FOR EDGE AND CUT A WEDGE. FLIP IT AGAIN AND CUT ANOTHER WEDGE. REPEAT TO PRODUCE THE NUMBER NEEDED.

5-19 Wedges can be rapidly cut with a radial-arm saw.

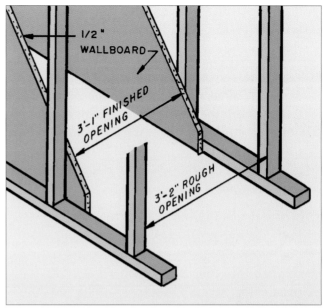

1/2" WALLBOARD

3'-1" FINISHED OPENING

3'-2" ROUGH OPENING

5-20 This framing allows one inch for the wallboard and one inch of space to help install a 36-inch stair.

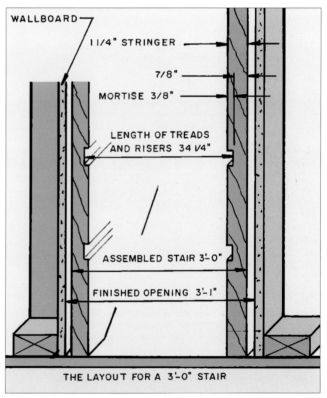

WALLBOARD

1 1/4" STRINGER

7/8"

MORTISE 3/8"

LENGTH OF TREADS AND RISERS 34 1/4"

ASSEMBLED STAIR 3'-0"

FINISHED OPENING 3'-1"

THE LAYOUT FOR A 3'-0" STAIR

5-21 How to determine the length of the treads and risers for a housed stringer stair.

4. Place the stringers on sawhorses or two work-benches (**5-22**). They should be secured so they cannot move.

5. Glue the top and bottom treads in place. Apply glue liberally in the tread mortise, and wedge. Insert the tread and tap a wedge lightly in the mortise on each side. Tap the tread board until it fits snuggly against the nosing of the mortise before you give the wedge its final, securing blow.

6. Secure the end of the tread to the stringer by installing one wood screw into the nosing and two more along the tread. Drill pilot holes through the stringer and anchor holes in the tread. Then secure the screws, which should pull the tread tight against the bottom of the mortise (**5-23**). You do not need to screw the risers to the stringer. If the stringer is left exposed to view, you can counterbore the screw and glue a wood plug over it.

7. Check to see that the assembly is square. You can check the tread-to-stringer for squareness with a framing square. Measure the diagonals from opposite corners, as shown in **5-22**. They should be the same length. If they are not, apply pressure along the long diagonal until they are square. Then clamp the stringers to the sawhorses or workbenches. You can use cabinetmakers, long bar clamps to help hold the unit during assembly.

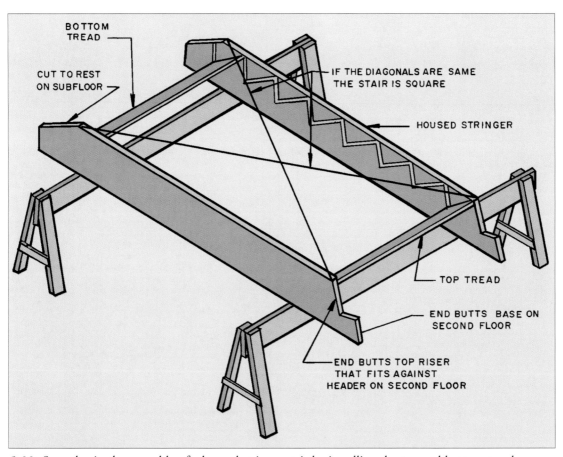

5-22 Some begin the assembly of a housed stringer stair by installing the top and bottom treads. Some install a couple in the middle of the stair next, to firm up the assembly.

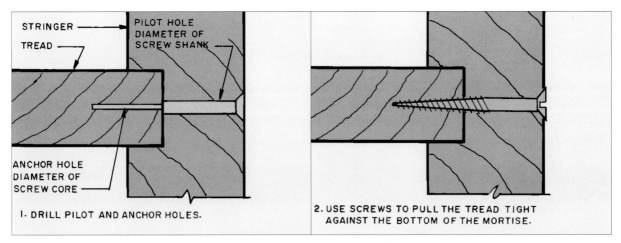

STRINGER
TREAD
PILOT HOLE DIAMETER OF SCREW SHANK
ANCHOR HOLE DIAMETER OF SCREW CORE

1. DRILL PILOT AND ANCHOR HOLES.

2. USE SCREWS TO PULL THE TREAD TIGHT AGAINST THE BOTTOM OF THE MORTISE.

5-23 You can use screws to pull the tread firmly against the bottom of the mortise.

8. Now install all the remaining treads. Some builders prefer to install one or two in the center to help hold the assembly square. Remember, the back edge of the tread or wedge should not project over the riser mortise. If it does, you cannot slide the riser in place. Check this before gluing and wedging the treads. Refer back to **5-18** on page 66.

9. Install the top and bottom risers by gluing and wedging, the same as you did the treads. Some prefer to install two screws through the stringer into the end of the risers.

The top riser may be a different width from the others. This depends upon the conditions of the floor at the top of the stair. Two conditions are shown in **5-24.**

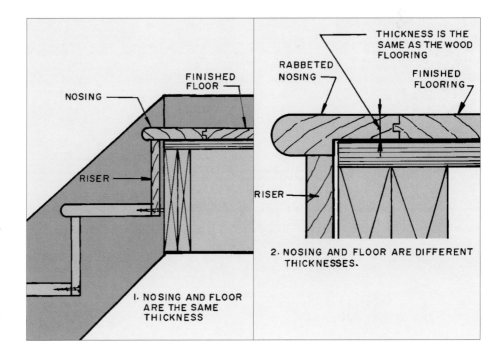

NOSING
FINISHED FLOOR
RISER

1. NOSING AND FLOOR ARE THE SAME THICKNESS

RABBETED NOSING
THICKNESS IS THE SAME AS THE WOOD FLOORING
FINISHED FLOORING
RISER

2. NOSING AND FLOOR ARE DIFFERENT THICKNESSES.

5-24 The treatment of the nosing and thickness of the finished wood floor at the second level will influence the width of the top riser.

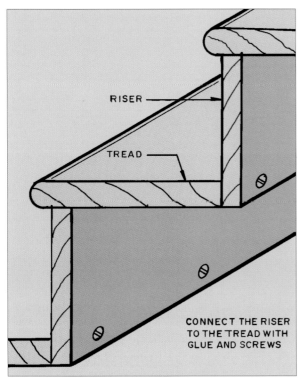

5-25 Glue and screw the riser to the treads.

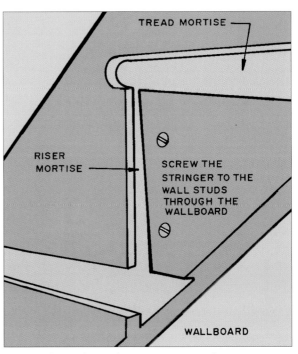

5-26 When a housed stringer is part of an open stair, the housed stringer against a wall can be screwed into the wall studs.

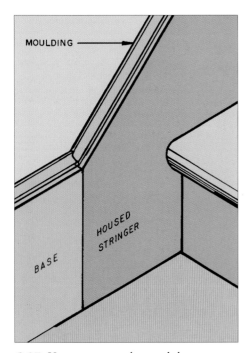

5-27 You can cover the crack between the stringer and the wallboard with a small molding.

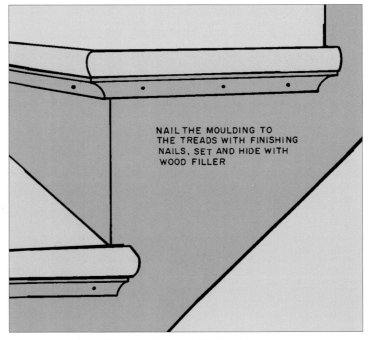

5-28 A small molding can be nailed below the tread to cover the crack with the skirtboard. Nail to the tread so that any movement will not reveal the crack.

10. Now install the remaining treads.

11. With wood screws join the bottom edge of the riser to the back of the tread. Drill pilot holes every 8 inches through the risers and anchor holes into the tread (5-25).

12. Finally, install several glue blocks as shown in Chapter 4 on page 50.

INSTALLING THE ASSEMBLED STAIR

Let the assembled stair sit overnight so the glue has a chance to cure. It is heavy, so it will take several people to lift it into the stairwell. To install the assembled stair:

1. Raise it up into the stairwell. Place the top riser against the header or hangerboard. You may want to nail 2 × 4 blocking on the subfloor at the bottom to keep the stair from sliding.

2. Once it is in place it should be leveled. It may be necessary to shim it out behind the top riser to get it level and aligned with the subfloor or finished floor at the second level. Be certain it is centered on the stairwell so that you have any needed clearance on the sides for drywall. Now secure the stringers to the hangerboard with screws.

3. Secure the bottom end of the stringers to the subfloor if it sits on top of it. You can use 2 × 4 blocking nailed behind the riser to the stringers and the floor.

4. If the drywall is in place, drive screws through the stringer below the treads and behind the risers into each stud. You may not be able to hit every stud, but screw into as many as possible (5-26).

5. You will most likely want to install a notched stringer in the center of the stair if it is 36 inches wide or wider.

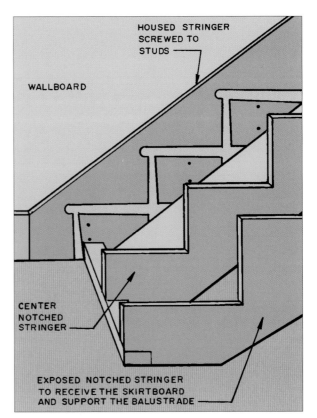

5-29 A stair with a housed stringer used on a stair with one side open will use two notched stringers.

6. After the stair is in place and the drywall installed, you may want to install a small molding along the top of the stringer to cover any crack at the wall (5-27).

A small molding can be nailed below each tread to cover the crack with the skirtboard (5-28). It can also be nailed along the top of the riser to cover any crack produced if you butted these rather than used a tongue-and-groove joint.

Housed stringers are also used on stairs with one side open and one closed. The housed stringer is placed on the closed wall and secured to the studs. Notched stringers are installed on the open side of the stair and, when required, in the center (5-29). The design of the stringers and installation is the same as discussed for housed and notched stringers. A beautiful finished stair of this type is shown in 5-6 on page 62.

L-Shaped & U-Shaped Stairs & Landings

6-1 This impressive stairway uses a landing that turns it into a U-shape.

Courtesy Designed Stairs, Inc. 1-877-4Stairs

L-shaped and U-shaped stairs use a landing partway up the flight to change their direction. The landing must be able to provide width and length to meet codes and support both flights. In **6-1** and **6-2** are examples of these stairs.

BUILDING LANDINGS

A landing is a platform installed in a flight of stairs that breaks it into two or more flights. It serves to give a resting place in a long flight.

Building codes specify that a total rise of 12 feet in or more should have a landing. In general a landing is placed about in the middle of the flight (**6-1**). However, available floor space may require one flight to be longer than the other. This frequently occurs when building L-shaped and U-shaped stairs (**6-2**). Some codes will have a limit on the minimum number of risers that are acceptable in a flight. Be certain to check your local code. Typically at least three risers are considered minimum and 18 risers maximum in a single flight of stairs.

For residential construction the landing must be as wide as the stair and at least 36 inches in the line of travel, but need not be over 48 inches in straight stairs.

To determine the height of the landing, note the number of risers specified on the architectural drawing for each flight and the size of the risers. If this is not given, measure the total rise floor to floor and calculate the riser size as explained in Chapter 2.

LANDINGS
IN STRAIGHT STAIRS

Landings in straight stairs are usually placed near the center of the flight. Using the unit rise, figure the landing height by allowing about half the risers below the landing. Seldom do these come out even, so one flight will usually have one more risers than the other. For an example, look at the illustration in **6-3.** In this example the stair has a total rise of 144 inches and 21 risers at $6^{27}/_{32}$ inches. To decide the height of the landing determine if it is to be near the center of the flight. In this case, with 21 risers it was decided to put 10 risers in the first flight and 11 inches the top flight. The height of the landing from the subfloor is 10 risers × $6^{27}/_{32}$ inches or 68⅜ inches.

6-2 An L-shaped stairway lets you fit the stair along a wall that is a bit short for a straight stair. It also adds an attractive architectural feature to the room.

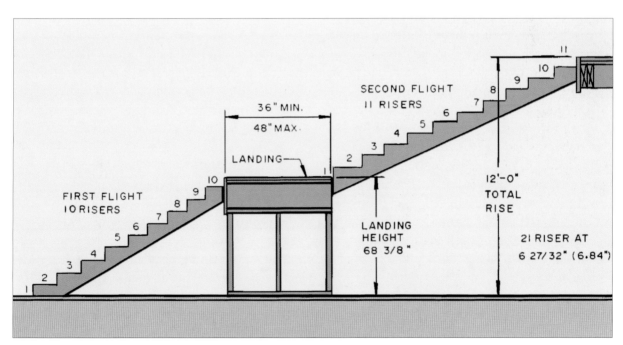

6-3 A typical stair layout for a building with 12 foot ceilings that requires a landing.

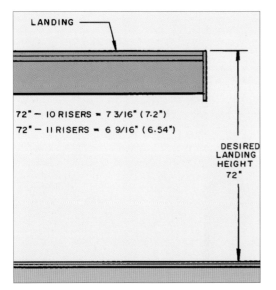

$72" - 10\ RISERS = 7\ 3/16" (7.2")$
$72" - 11\ RISERS = 6\ 9/16" (6.54")$

6-4 You can adjust the number and size of the risers to get a landing exactly in the center of the stair, but be careful you do not violate the codes as you do it.

6-5 A landing should be as long as the width of stair but never less than 36 inches,

Should you want to make the landing exactly halfway, locate it in the center of the total rise and calculate the stair risers from that location. In the above example the rise to the center of the total rise is 144 ÷ 2 = 72 inches. You can use 10 risers 7³⁄₁₆ inches high in each flight (6-4) if codes permit, or 11 risers 6⁹⁄₁₆ inches in each flight.

Remember, the tread, width, and height are the same for all treads and risers on both flights.

You must decide on the width of the landing. This will vary a little depending upon some design decisions and whether the landing is closed on both sides or open on one or both sides. If the stair is closed on both sides, the landing will be the same width as the stairwell. When the drywall is installed it will be on top of the landing. If it is open on one or both sides, you will need to allow for the design and placement of a balustrade.

The length of the landing will be at least 36 inches and will include the hangerboard if one is used (6-5). The decking will extend over the hangerboard and, if it is to be carpeted, will extend outward, forming the nosing. It can be rounded in the same manner as the treads. If a nosing is used, the landing decking is notched to accommodate the skirt in the same manner as for stair construction at the top of the stair. Review Chapters 4 and 5 for construction details.

Another factor is how the second flight is connected to the landing. If it is hung with metal joist hangers, the 36 inches length will be used. If it rests on top of the landing, you must add the additional length used for this connection (6-6).

PLANNING AN L-SHAPED
OR U-SHAPED STAIR

The layout principles are the same as described earlier in Chapter 4 for a straight stair. They include determining tread and riser sizes, how to handle differences in the total rise caused by the addition of solid wood flooring on one or both levels, and working the design in the amount of floor space available. The layout of the stringer is also the same.

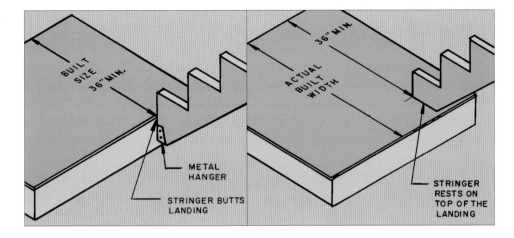

6-6 The stringer of the second flight can be mounted on top of the landing-or you can butt it against the landing, hanging it with a metal hanger. The method used influences the size of the landing.

Frequently the landing is near the center of the total rise. However, space limitations often will not permit this. Check your local code to see the minimum number of risers allowed in one flight. Often the smaller of the flights must have at least three risers.

A design layout for an L-shaped stair is shown in **6-7**. In this example the landing was placed at the center of the total rise. The calculations are the same as those described for the straight stair in Chapter 4, using the Pythagorean theorem to figure the sringer layout.

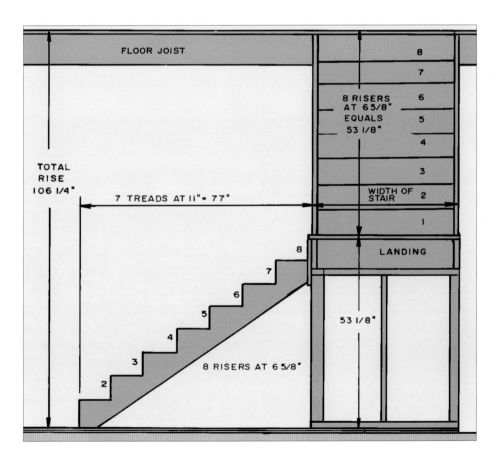

6-7 An L-shaped stair design with the landing in the center of the total rise.

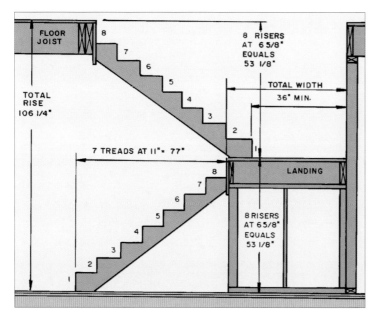

6-8 A U-shaped stair design with the landing in the center of the total rise is figured in the same manner as the L-shaped stair.

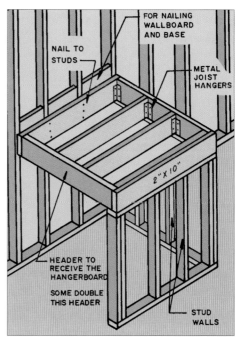

6-10 Framing for a landing on a straight stairway.

6-9 This stairway approaches a landing from which stairs are run from the left and right sides. Notice the wrought-iron balustrade.

Courtesy Designed Stairs, Inc. 1-877-4Stairs

The planning for a U-shaped stair with the same conditions is shown in **6-8**. The major difference is figuring the length of the landing.

LANDINGS FOR L-SHAPED & U-SHAPED STAIRS

The landing for an L-shaped stair is figured as just described for the straight stair in **6-3**, **6-4**, and **6-5**. The difference is that the upper flight comes off the side of the landing, making a 90-degree turn. The landing must be as wide as the stair. However, it could be longer in one direction if desired. It can also turn right or left or both ways, as shown in **6-9**. The length of the landing must include space for the stringer to rest on top of it, if this is the required design (**6-6**).

A U-shaped stair landing is similar to those used on straight and L-shaped stairs. The difference is that it has a longer landing, enabling both flights to leave from the same side. As with the other stairs, the landing does not necessarily have to be in the middle of the flight but is more effective if it approaches the middle. If the stringers rest on top of the landing, the width must be increased to allow the code-required minimum plus this extra width.

FRAMING THE LANDING

Framing for a landing for a straight stair is shown in **6-10**. The platform is built much like the floor framing. The joists used are typically 2 × 10. These provide a stiff, solid base for the landing deck and finished floor.

The joists that run along wall studs are nailed to them. The end joists are usually single, but can be doubled fot extra strength or a long span.

The platform can be supported by posts or a stud wall. The wall provides greater protection from racking and can have 1 × 4 diagonal braces added to ensure rigidity. Notice the 2 × 10 blocking between the studs at the wall, intersecting the landing. This provides a nailing surface for the drywall and baseboard.

A hangerboard is nailed to the side of the landing and the stringers are secured to it. They are set in place and firmed up with a kicker, as described for installing straight stairs.

The landing is covered with ¾-inch-thick plywood. Then the stringers for the second flight are installed. If they rest on top of the landing, a kicker is used, too. Remember to leave space between the stringers and the stud wall for the drywall and a skirtboard if notched stringers are used. A complete installation is shown in **6-11**.

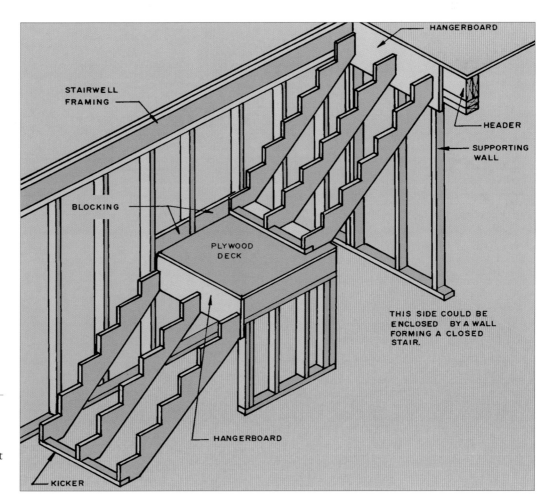

6-11 A completed stair frame for a straight stair with a landing.

The framing for an L-shaped stair is in **6-12**. On this example the stringers of the second flight rest on top of the platform, so it was made longer to hold them. The construction of the landing is similar to that shown for a straight stair (**6-10**).

A landing for a U-shaped stair is built in the same manner. It turns the stair 180 degrees. Since it has a long doubled header joist it could be quite bouncy unless a supporting wall is built below it. Refer to **6-13** for details. The platform framing is shown in **6-14**.

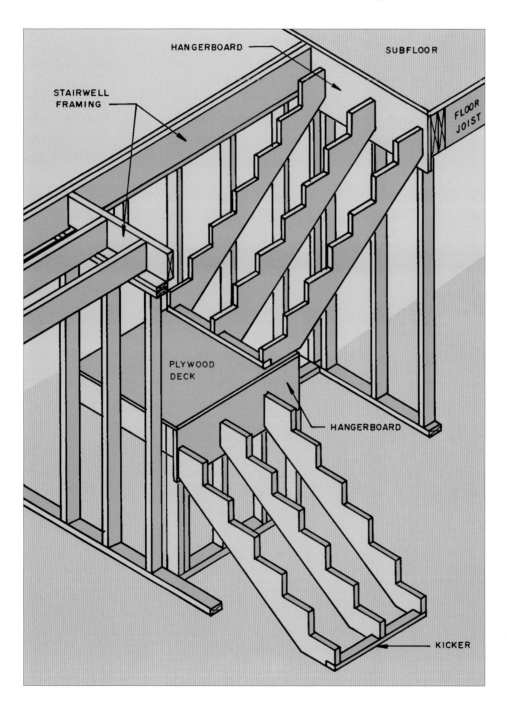

6-12 A typical framed L-shaped stair.

6-13 Typical landing and stringer framing for a U-shaped stair.

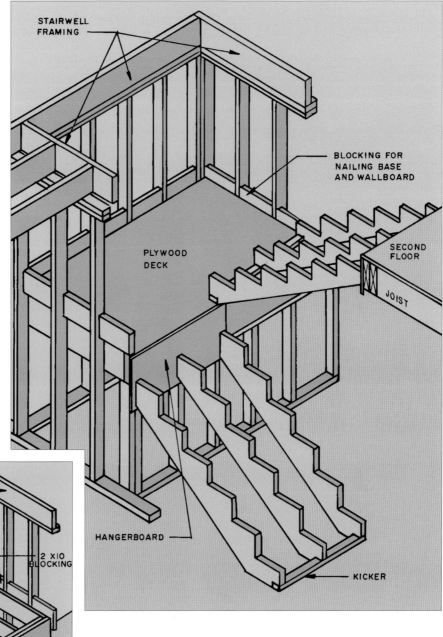

STAIRWELL FRAMING

BLOCKING FOR NAILING BASE AND WALLBOARD

PLYWOOD DECK

SECOND FLOOR

JOIST

HANGERBOARD

KICKER

STAIRWELL FRAMING

2 X10 BLOCKING

2 X 10 HEADER

HANGERBOARD TO BE NAILED TO THIS HEADER

6-14 (Left) One way to frame a landing for a U-shaped stair.

L-SHAPED & U-SHAPED STAIRS & LANDINGS

On-site carpenter-built L-shaped stair framing is shown in **6-15** through **6-18**. The framing for a landing on a U-shaped stair is shown in **6-19**.

Both L-shaped and U-shaped stairs can be turned with winders. The basic landing is built the same as for these stairs, using the landing as the direction-turning feature.

6-16 A view of the landing and stringers after the wallboard has been installed. Notice the temporary treads and the mess from finishing the drywall. The bottom has also been covered with wallboard so that the floor area below can serve as storage.

6-15 This shows the stringers in place hung on the hangerboard at the landing. Notice the 2 × 4 spacer on each side to allow for the wallboard and skirtboard.

6-17 (Right) This side view shows the second flight of the L-shaped stair. The stringers rest on top of the landing. Notice the wall framing. This will be covered with wallboard, producing an open side. See 6-18 for the wallboard application.

6-18 The wallboard has been installed on the open side of the second flight. The finished stair will have an attractive balustrade installed along this open side.

6-19 This shows the rear of a landing for a U-shaped stair. The long landing has been supported by partitions on the side and rear.

Courtesy Designed Stairs, Inc. 1-877-4Stairs

6-20 This stair uses winders to make a 90-degree turn.

TURNING STAIRS WITH WINDERS

Winders are used when an L-shaped or U-shaped stair must be used and space is limited (6-20). They save space because of the landing area, which accounts for one tread providing three landing treads on L-shaped stairs and six treads on U-shaped stairs (6-21). Winders can also be used to turn a stair on an acute angle (less than 90 degrees), as shown in 6-22.

Whenever possible, avoid the use of winders. They have a triangular tread and if you walk on the narrow end you are likely to slip and fall.

Building codes have very specific requirements for the design of winders. Before designing your winders, consult your local building codes. Typically they will require the winder treads to be at least 6 inches wide on the narrow end and at least 9 inches wide a distance of 12 inches in from this narrow end, as shown in 6-23. The length of sides needed to lay out the 6 inches side on a 45-degree angle is found using the Pythagorean theorem for a right triangle, as shown in 6-24.

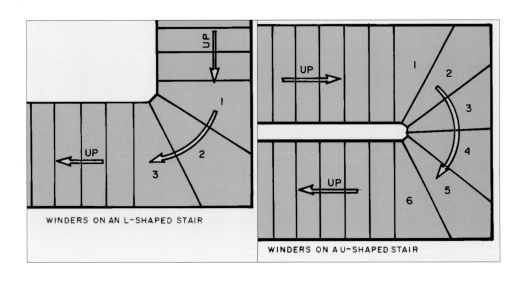

WINDERS ON AN L-SHAPED STAIR

WINDERS ON A U-SHAPED STAIR

6-21 Winders can be used on stairs where space is limited. These turn angles of 90 degrees and 180 degrees.

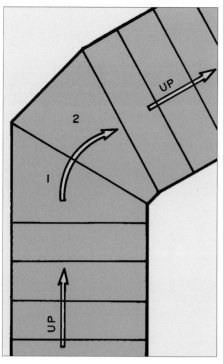

6-22 Winders can also be used on stairs turning acute angles.

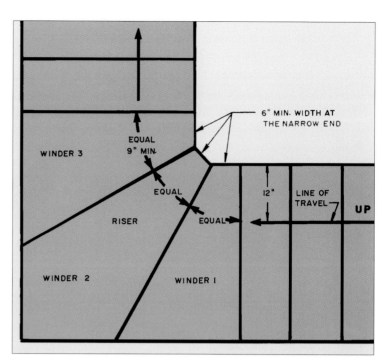

6-23 Many codes require that the narrow end of a winder tread be at least 6 inches and the tread be at least 9 inches, one foot in from the narrow end.

A winder requires three treads to turn a 90-degree corner. These are figured in as normal treads as the stair is designed and those remaining in the total stair are divided between the lower and upper flights. The height of the platform and its construction is the same as for an L-shaped stair with a landing. After you construct the landing and the carriages for the two flights you can build the winder risers and treads.

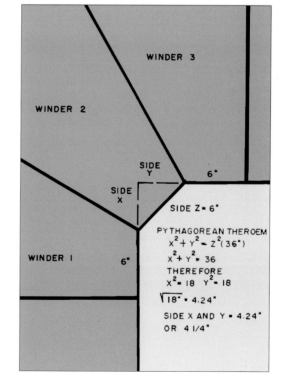

6-24 The points forming the end of the 6-inch narrow end of the center winder tread can be found using the Pythagorean theorem.

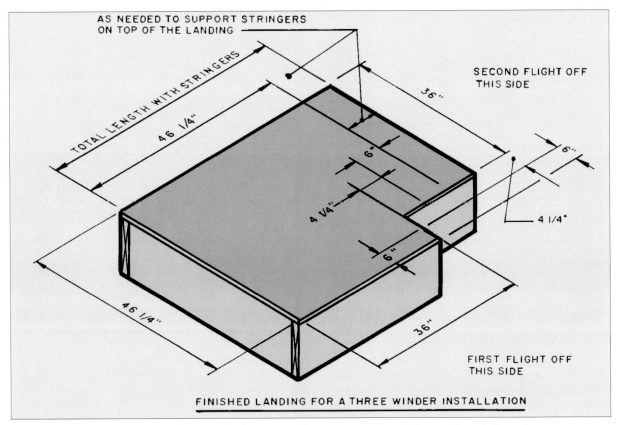

AS NEEDED TO SUPPORT STRINGERS ON TOP OF THE LANDING

TOTAL LENGTH WITH STRINGERS

46 1/4"

SECOND FLIGHT OFF THIS SIDE

36"

6"

4 1/4"

6"

6"

4 1/4"

46 1/4"

36"

FIRST FLIGHT OFF THIS SIDE

FINISHED LANDING FOR A THREE WINDER INSTALLATION

6-25 The landing for the winders must be large enough to support the winder treads and the stringers.

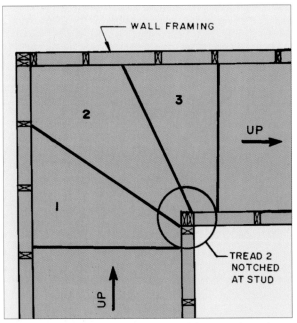

WALL FRAMING

3

2

UP

1

UP

TREAD 2 NOTCHED AT STUD

6-26 This is a typical winder tread layout when the center tread is notched at the corner wall stud.

LAYING OUT
THE WINDERS

As you design the layout of the winders, the landing platform will have to be large enough to carry the stair width plus extra surface to allow you to lay out the winders to meet the code. The layout for a stair 36 inches wide is shown in **6-25**. The landing must be wide enough for the stair stringers and to turn the corner, and there should be allowance for the second flight to rest on top of the landing if this is the plan. Refer back to **6-24** for the dimensions at the corner.

This landing produces a notched second winder tread on the narrow end, as shown in the layout in **6-26**.

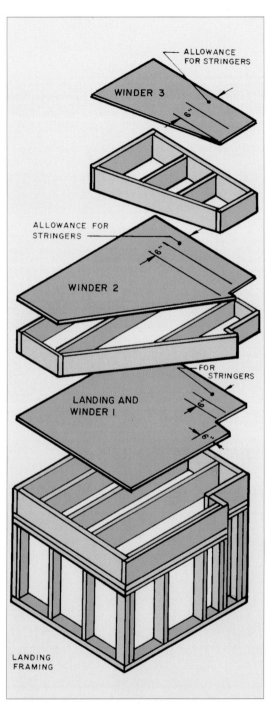

6-27 Each winder is built using a frame of 2-inch stock and covered with ¾-inch plywood. It is best if they are glued and nailed with ring-shank nails.

BUILDING THE WINDERS

The winders can be built using special stringers similar to those used for straight stairs. However, it is easier to build each step as a separate unit and mount one on top of the other (6-27).

Use two-inch stock cut to the required width for the riser board. Remember, a ¾-inch-thick plywood tread is included in the riser height. Assemble by gluing and nailing the plywood to the riser frame. Set the heads of the nails so they will not penetrate the carpet pad. Each riser can be secured to the one below by gluing and toenailing or screwing from below (6-28).

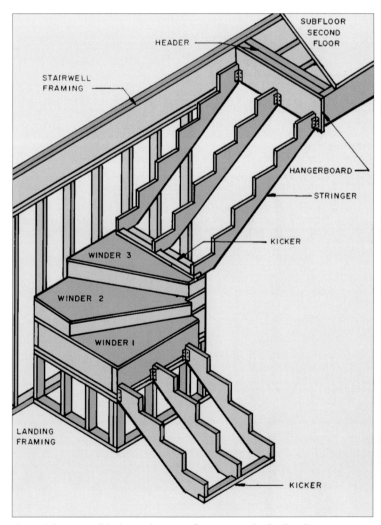

6-28 The assembled winder stair framing with the landing, winders, and stringers in place.

6-29 This flight runs to the landing upon which the winders have been built.

In **6-29** through **6-33** are views of an example of the carpenter-built rough stair framing for winders.

A typical winder layout for a stair turning an angle that is less than 90 degrees is shown in **6-33**. Notice that the two winders butt the wall before the stair is turned. A stair turning an angleless than 90 degree is framed in a manner similar to that shown in **6-27** and **6-28** on page 85.

A finished stairway is shown in **6-34** on page 88.

6-30 A view of the winders turning a 90-degree corner. This stair requires less floor space than the L-shaped stair.

6-31 The winders after the wall-board has been installed. The wallboard comes down on top of the edges of the winders.

6-32 This view of the finished rough winders shows how the stair turns the 90-degree corner.

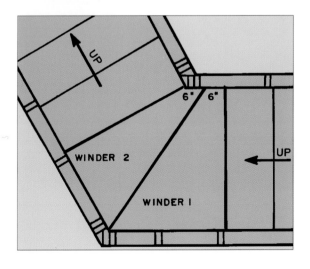

6-33 A typical winder tread lay-out for a stair with an angle less than 90 degrees. Notice that the narrow ends of the winder treads butt the wall along the lower flight.

6-34 This stairway uses winders to turn a corner less than 90 degrees.

MANUFACTURED STAIRS

Manufactured stairs are widely used for straight, L-shaped, U-shaped, curved, and spiral stairs. The manufacturer produces the stairs under controlled conditions in his factory. The precision cutting tools and assembly and clamping devices permit a high-quality product to be produced. Manufacturers receive information from the building contractor concerning the conditions into which the stair must fit. This includes the floor-to-ceiling height, supporting walls, and finished flooring to be used.

The manufacturer will also provide the many parts for the balustrade, cut so that they can be easily assembled on the site. Following is an example of the installation of one such product.

In **6-35** the assembled stair section is delivered to the site ready to be installed. In some cases the manufacturer will send technicians to install the stair. Otherwise it is set in place by a local stair contractor.

6-35 The assembled flight is moved to the building. Notice that the stair is covered to protect the treads and risers.

The contractor has prepared the framing to receive the stair, which is built to install in the conditions specified (**6-36**). In this example an L-shaped stair has been ordered, so the upper flight is leveled and secured to the header. This requires only a hammer, drill, and level (**6-37**).

Now the lower flight moves into the room. Notice the treads are covered to prevent damage (**6-38**). Lift the lower section into place and connect it to the upper section.

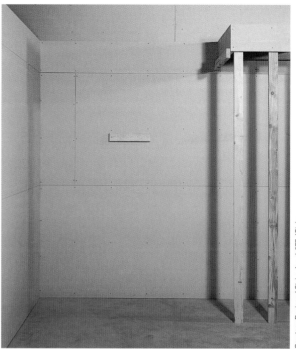

6-36 (Right) The on-site framing crew prepares for the stair. The dimensions are sent to the manufacturer. Since this is to be an L-shaped stair, the landing could be built now or after the stair is installed.

6-37 Set the upper section in place. It is secured to the header on the second-floor joists.

6-38 Move the second flight into position.

6-39 Raise the lower section into position and connect it to the upper flight at the landing newel. In this case the landing is to be built after the stair is installed.

Notice in **6-39** that the landing newel is in place and connected to the upper flight. The landing is built using conventional on-site framing. It can be built after the flights are installed or be built beforehand with the dimensions sent to the manufacturer.

6-40 Install the other newels using prepositioned fasteners and secure the handrail.

Finally, the other newels are installed using predrilled and installed connectors and the handrail is placed between them (**6-40**).

Courtesy Designed Stairs, Inc. 1-877-4Stairs

6-41 Now set the balusters in the predrilled handrails and treads.

6-42 The fully assembled stair ready to have the landing and any partitions below built.

The balusters are set in predrilled handrails and treads (**6-41**) and the stair is ready for installing the walls below and finished (**6-42**).

Photos showing the erection of manufactured curved stairway are provided in Chapter 7.

Considerable bracing and support structure is used. Spiral stairways are also manufactured and delivered to the job. Some are assembled after delivery, while others are assembled before they are shipped. These are also shown in Chapter 7.

Curved & Spiral Stairways

A curved stairway provides an attractive alternative to the L-shaped stair. The treads are of normal size, providing better foot support than stairs with winders. They take up no more floor space than most L-shaped stairs and, best of all, provide a dramatic architectural feature to the entrance foyer as seen in **7-1**.

The curved stair is available from stairway manufacturers who supply the entire structure and send technicians to the job to assist with the installation (**7-2** through **7-4**).

An example of a possible layout of a curved stair, with a comparison with the L-shaped stair with a landing, is in **7-5**.

7-2 The manufacturer assembles the stairs in sections in the factory and ships these to the job. This provides quality construction and speeds the erection on the job.

7-1 A curved stairway as part of the entrance foyer provides an attractive architectural feature to the home.

7-3 The curved sections are installed and securely braced during the process.

7-4 The final section is in place and the bullnose at the floor is set.

7-5 Curved stairs take about the same amount of floor area as L-shaped stairs.

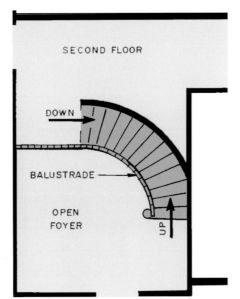

SECOND FLOOR

DOWN

BALUSTRADE

OPEN FOYER

UP

SECOND FLOOR

DOWN

BALUSTRADE

OPEN FOYER

UP

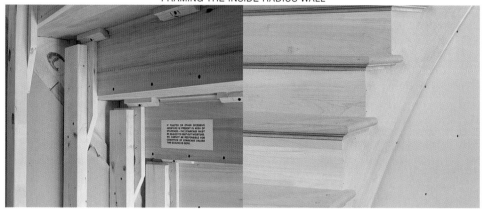

Courtesy Arcways, Inc. 1-800-558-5096

7-6 The inside radius wall faces the foyer and has the exposed stringer, treads, and balustrade. Notice the use of glue blocks and blocking. The risers are screwed to the back edge of the treads.

The installation of a curved stair involves constructing the outside and inside radius wall below the stair after it has been installed. Construction details for stairs provided by one manufacturer are shown in 7-6 and 7-7.

Detailed drawings are available, so the design can be checked by the contractor on site to confirm that the stair will be built to the conditions that exist when the stair will be installed.

The manufacturer of the curved stairway will request information about the existing floor-to-ceiling height and the area on the floor plan where the stairway will be constructed. A drawing detailing information about the stair is provided. In 7-8 is part of the total drawing that shows the layout of the proposed stairway. Notice that the manufacturer supplies the balustrade and stair rail

that are installed by a local stair-builder. This large drawing also has section drawings showing the construction details.

A design for a curved stair similar to a typical L-shaped stair with winders is shown in 7-9. It uses curved stringers and does not use a landing in the curved section. A straight flight is built at each end, as needed.

An even more eye-catching design uses a 180-degree turn with the treads narrowed at the inside radius wall and regular rectangular treads at the beginning and end, as needed, to complete the rise (7-10). Curved walls called radius walls are built below the curved stairway in this and the other designs. Refer to 7-6 and 7-7. In 7-11 you can see a completed curved stairway. The wall below is the inside-radius wall.

Courtesy Arcways, Inc. 1-800-558-5096

7-7 The outside radius wall encloses the back side of the curved stair. Notice the connections between the stringer and the wall studs.

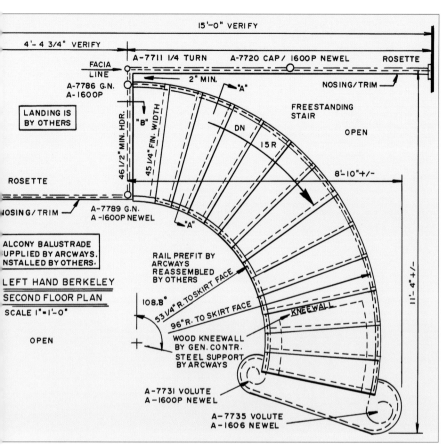

15'-0" VERIFY

4'- 4 3/4" VERIFY

FACIA LINE

A-7786 G.N.
A-1600P

A-7711 1/4 TURN   A-7720 CAP/ 1600P NEWEL   ROSETTE

2" MIN.   "A"   NOSING/TRIM

LANDING IS BY OTHERS

46 1/2" MIN. HDR.   45 1/4" FIN. WIDTH   "B"

FREESTANDING STAIR

DN   OPEN

15R

ROSETTE

8'-10"+/-

NOSING/TRIM   A-7789 G.N.
A-1600P NEWEL   "A"

BALCONY BALUSTRADE SUPPLIED BY ARCWAYS. INSTALLED BY OTHERS.

LEFT HAND BERKELEY SECOND FLOOR PLAN

SCALE 1"=1'-0"

OPEN

RAIL PREFIT BY ARCWAYS REASSEMBLED BY OTHERS

53 1/4" R. TO SKIRT FACE

108.8°   96"R. TO SKIRT FACE

WOOD KNEEWALL BY GEN. CONTR.
STEEL SUPPORT BY ARCWAYS

KNEEWALL

11'-4" +/-

A-7731 VOLUTE
A-1600P NEWEL

A-7735 VOLUTE
A-1606 NEWEL

7-8 This stair layout is part of a large drawing that gives detailed information about the design of the curved stair.   Courtesy Arcways, Inc. 1-800-558-5096

Courtesy Designed Stairs, Inc. 1-877-4Stairs

7-11 This completed circular stairway starts with a bullnose starting step and three regular treads before it begins to curve. Notice the rounded inside-radius wall below the exposed skirtboard.

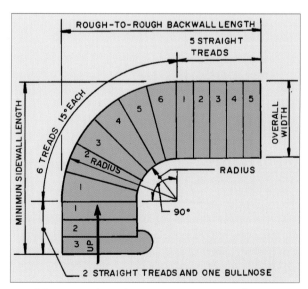

ROUGH-TO-ROUGH BACKWALL LENGTH

5 STRAIGHT TREADS

MINIMUN SIDEWALL LENGTH

6 TREADS 15° EACH

2 RADIUS

RADIUS

OVERALL WIDTH

6   1   2   3   4   5

90°

2 STRAIGHT TREADS AND ONE BULLNOSE

7-9 This curved 90-degree stairway serves the same purpose as the L-shaped one with a landing. The on-site space available and total rise must be carefully evaluated before the stair is manufactured.

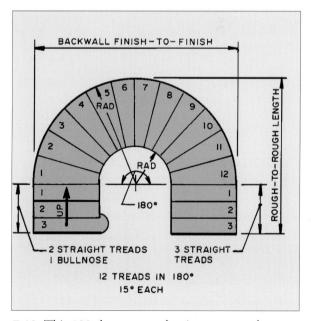

BACKWALL FINISH-TO-FINISH

RAD

RAD

180°

ROUGH-TO-ROUGH LENGTH

2 STRAIGHT TREADS 1 BULLNOSE

3 STRAIGHT TREADS

12 TREADS IN 180° 15° EACH

7-10 This 180-degree curved stairway serves the same purpose as the U-shaped stair with its landing.

CURVED & SPIRAL STAIRWAYS

7-12 Spiral stairs are in the form of a helix. This all-wood stair provides access to the above level and requires very little floor space.

CODES FOR CURVED STAIRS

Building codes typically specify that curved (circular) stairs have a minimum tread depth of 11 and a maximum riser height of 7 inches. The small radius of the stairway must be at least twice the width. The minimum tread depth measured 12 inches in from the narrow end of the tread, should be 11 inches. Check your local codes for their requirements.

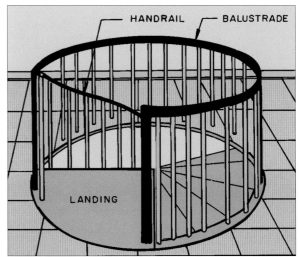

7-14 The spiral stair opening must be fully protected to avoid accidental stepping into the opening. This round balustrade is strong and decorative.

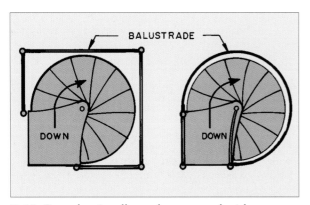

7-13 Round stairwells can be protected with rectangular or round balustrades.

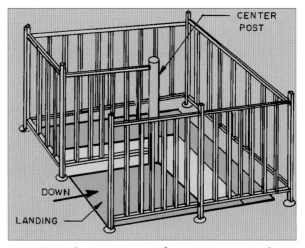

7-15 Some homeowners prefer to use a rectangular balustrade around a rectangular or circular opening for a spiral stair at the second floor level.

SPIRAL STAIRWAYS

Spiral stairs are circular in plan, having treads that wind around a center structural pole. They are available in hardwoods such as oak, mahogany, maple, walnut, and cherry (**7-12**). They are also available with steel treads and framing. The balustrades are typically brass, steel, or hardwood. Wood treads can be installed over the steel treads if you want a contrast of materials and color.

The stairwell opening is enclosed with a railing designed to match the balustrade. Circular stairwells can be protected with either a round or rectangular balustrade (**7-13**) around rectangular or round openings (**7-14**and **7-15**).

Installation instructions are provided by the manufacturer and some have videotapes available. A typical installation sequence for a metal stair is shown in **7-16** through **7-21**. While specifications will vary with the type and design of the unit, this procedure is representative. Some spiral stairs are shipped assembled.

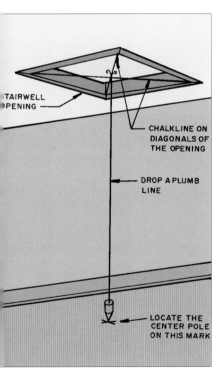

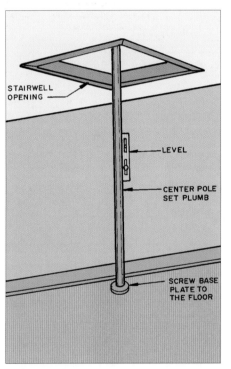

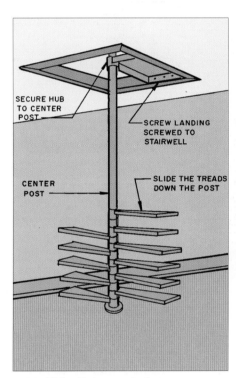

7-16 Steps to installation of a typical steel spiral stair (7-16 through 7-21). Exact details will vary depending on the manufacturer. A Prepare the stairwell in the second floor as specified by the spiral stair manufacturer. See Chapter 3 for framing information. Locate the center of the stairwell on the floor with a chalkline.

7-17 Install the center pole. Center it on the opening and keep it plumb. Screw the base plate to the floor. Drill pilot holes and use screws in wood floors. Secure to concrete floors with masonry anchors.

7-18 Slide all the treads down the pole. Be certain the top of the treads is facing up. Then install the landing plate in the stairwell. Position it so you can leave and enter the stair from the side planned. The landing is usually secured to the center pole with set screws and to the sides of the stairwell with wood screws.

Further steps in the installation of a typical steel spiral stair are shown in **7-19 to 7-21.** A detail for a wood-framed spiral stair is seen in **7-22.**

As you plan for a spiral stairway consider the floor area available. The smallest stair requires a 42-inch square and some are as large as 72 inches. The larger the diameter, the easier it is to ascend and descend the stair. When you order a spiral stair, notify the manufacturer of your local code requirements so the unit as built will meet this code. Typically, stairs with diameters 5 feet 6 inches and larger meet most codes. Those below this provide a *secondary access,* but a second code approved primary stair is required.

In **7-23** are shown the two commonly used spiral stairway layouts. One is ascended moving clockwise (also referred to as left-hand up) and the other is counterclockwise (also referred to as right-hand up). The number of treads varies with the height. The stairwell can be square or circular. You must plan how to place the stair so as to get on it conveniently on the first floor,

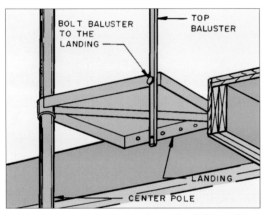

7-19 Connect a baluster from the balustrade surrounding the stairwell to the corner of the landing with the bolt provided.

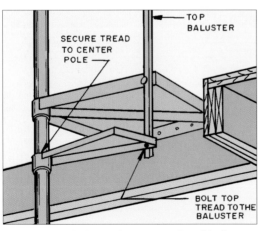

7-20 Then slide up the top tread and bolt it to the baluster and secure it to the post with the set screws. Check it with a level before tightening the set screws.

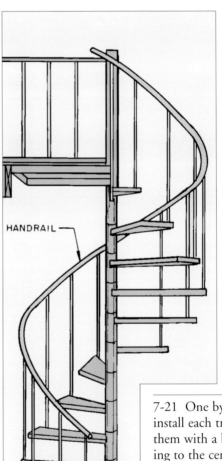

7-21 One by one raise and install each tread connecting them with a baluster and securing to the center post. Then bolt the plastic handrail to the bottom baluster and to each baluster on up the stair using the screws and connections provided. Let the handrail extend about 2 inches beyond the bottom and top balusters.

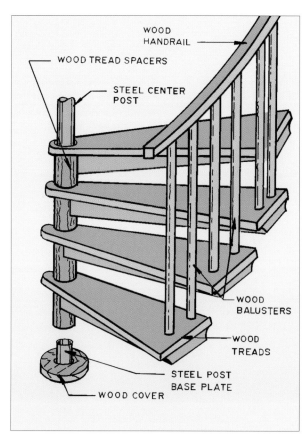

7-22 Wood-framed spiral stair details.

yet provide for the landing on the second floor and enable you to leave the stair safely. The stairwell is enclosed with a balustrade. Refer to **7-13**, **7-14**, and **7-15**.

CODES FOR SPIRAL STAIRWAYS

Spiral stairways are not to be used as the main means of egress, except when placed within a single dwelling unit. The minimum width is 26 inches and each tread must be 7½ inches wide at a point 12 inches from the narrow edge. The maximum rise is 9½ inches and all treads should be identical in size and shape. A minimum headroom of 6 feet 6 inches is required.

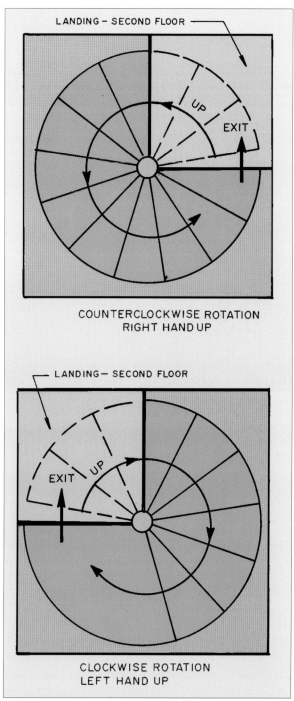

7-23 Spiral stairs are designed to rotate clockwise (left-hand up) and counterclockwise (right-hand up).

Installing the Ballustrade

While the balustrade provides the main decorative feature of the stair, it also is a major safety device. It must meet codes and be strong.

The two types of balustrade are the **post-to-post** and **over-the-post**. The **post-to-post** has the handrail butt the newel post as seen in **8-1.** The newel post usually has a decorative turning or finial at the top. The **over-the-post** system has the handrail on top of the post and connected to it with some type of fitting such as volutes, turnouts, opening caps, and up-easing gooseneck fittings (**8-2**).

The construction of the balustrade requires accurate measurements and careful work. There are a number of ways to do the job. Also the design of the stair will influence what technique you might use. A variation of balustrade construction is shown in **8-3.** It uses a large rectangular handrail and sturdy square balusters. This is an example of post-to-post construction. Another approach is to frame the balustrade area with studs and finish with drywall or some other wall finishes material. It will be topped off with a wood cap and a handrail can be added on top of the rail cap. Remember to keep the entire thing within the maximum and minimum heights allowed by codes (**8-4**). A handrail may be installed on the wall instead of the closed balustrade, if you prefer.

8-1 This is a post-to-post balustrade.

8-2 This over-the-post balustrade uses fittings to connect the handrail to the top of the newels.

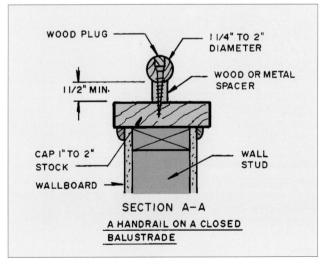

8-3 This balustrade is built using a wide rectangular handrail and sturdy rectangular balusters. This design uses a post-to-post construction.

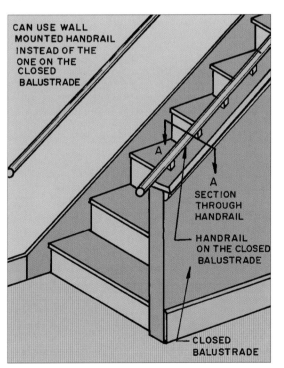

8-4 Closed balustrades can have a handrail mounted on top of the balustrade. Be certain that the height and handrail meet local codes. An alternative is to mount the handrail on the wall.

Typical framing for the closed balustrade is shown in **8-5**. An alternate design is shown in **8-6**; it requires that the handrail be on the wall.

8-5 This is the framing for a closed balustrade along the open side of a stair. The exposed studs will be covered with gypsum wallboard ,and a finished wood cap will be on top serving as a handrail.

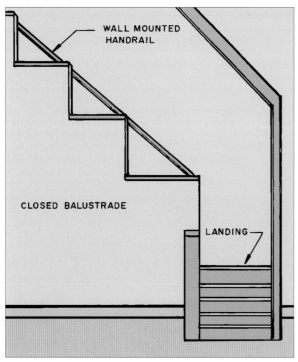

8-6 An alternate framing plan for a closed balustrade. Notice the handrail is mounted on the other wall.

LOCATING THE CENTERLINE

The balustrade is located by establishing its centerline. This is important because it locates the newel posts, which are the first part to be installed. The procedure for locating the centerline can vary, depending upon the construction of the stair and the preference of the stair builder. Following are several procedures used for stairs with straight handrails and no turnouts and volutes at the newel posts.

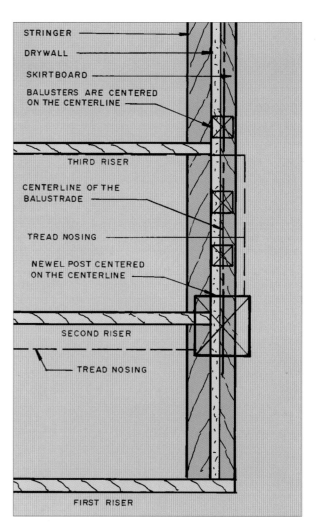

8-7 This stairway has the stringer covered with drywall over which a skirtboard has been installed. The centerline of the balustrade is the inner face of the skirtboard. The tread nosing extends beyond the riser and skirtboard.

If the stair stringer is covered with drywall and a skirtboard over this, the centerline is the inner face of the skirtboard (8-7). The newel post is notched to fit over the riser and stringer.

If the rough stringer has a skirtboard secured directly to it, the centerline of the balustrade could be the outer face of the skirtboard (8-8).

If the balustrade uses turnouts and volutes, the starting newel post is set on the starting step (8-9) and is not in line with the centerline of the balustrade. You can use a template supplied by the manufacturer to locate the newel post and any balusters that may be on the starting step (8-10), or make a template using the actual fitting as a pattern.

8-9 This beautiful balustrade uses a turnout to connect the handrail to the newel post. The post is set on the first tread, as is one baluster.

8-8 This stairway has a skirtboard covering the rough stringer. The centerline of the balustrade has been lined up with the outer face of the skirtboard. This permits the tread to butt the newel post on the side and back.

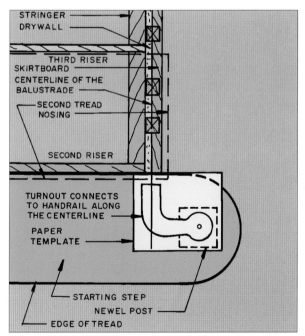

8-10 This shows how the turnout or volute is laid out from the centerline of the balustrade. It is essential to locate the newel post perfectly so the end of the turnout will line up with the end of the handrail.

8-11 The starting newel on this stairway is placed on the floor, butting the first riser.

8-12 This starting newel is placed against the second riser, allowing one tread to extend beyond it.

INSTALLING THE STARTING NEWEL

The starting newel is placed on the floor at the end of the stair (8-11) or at one tread in, butting the stringer at the second riser as seen in 8-12.

Stair builders use a number of ways to install the newel posts. The goal is to get them strong, because the entire balustrade relies on them for its strength. Following are some examples:

A starting newel mounted on the floor can extend through the subfloor and be bolted to a floor joist or blocking, as shown in 8-13 and 8-14. Bolts provide a more permanent

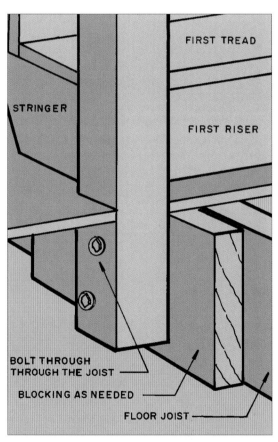

8-13 Run the newel post through the subfloor and bolt it to a floor joist if one is quite close.

connection than lag screws. Use washers under the heads and nuts. Remember that the center of the newel should line up with the centerline of the balustrade. The post can butt the riser or be notched to fit up over it a little (**8-15**).

In **8-16** the newel posts have been bolted to the stringer, wall, and landing framing. They are ready to have the handrail installed.

NOTCHING
THE NEWEL

Newel posts frequently have to be notched to fit over a tread so that their centerline is on the centerline of the balustrade **8-16**. They are carefully laid out, as shown in **8-15**.

8-16 The newel posts have been installed to the frame with bolts or lag screws. Now you can measure the length of the handrail and prepare it for the connector to join it to the newels. Notice the drawings on the sheet hanging on the wall.

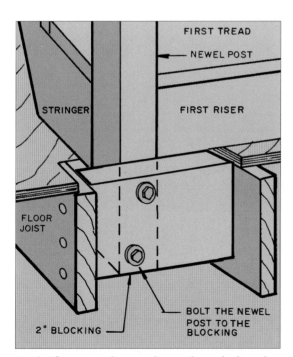

8-14 If you run the newel post through the sub-floor and there is no floor joist close to it, install blocking between the joists and bolt it to the blocking.

8-15 The newel post must often be notched to fit over the corner of a step so that the centerline lines up with the centerline of the balustrade. Here the top of the notch is being marked so the newel will fit over the tread.

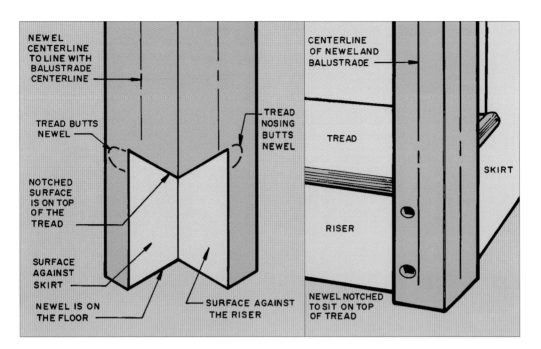

NEWEL CENTERLINE TO LINE WITH BALUSTRADE CENTERLINE

TREAD BUTTS NEWEL

TREAD NOSING BUTTS NEWEL

NOTCHED SURFACE IS ON TOP OF THE TREAD

SURFACE AGAINST SKIRT

NEWEL IS ON THE FLOOR

SURFACE AGAINST THE RISER

CENTERLINE OF NEWEL AND BALUSTRADE

TREAD

SKIRT

RISER

NEWEL NOTCHED TO SIT ON TOP OF TREAD

8-17 This notched starting newel fits over the tread and has its centerline matching the centerline of the balustrade.

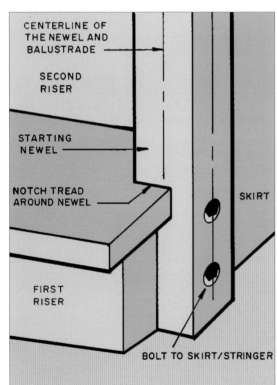

CENTERLINE OF THE NEWEL AND BALUSTRADE

SECOND RISER

STARTING NEWEL

NOTCH TREAD AROUND NEWEL

SKIRT

FIRST RISER

BOLT TO SKIRT/STRINGER

8-18 This newel post is bolted to the stringer and is notched to line it up with the centerline of the balustrade. The tread is notched around the newel. This will show gaps at the newel and does not produce the highest quality connection.

A layout for a starting newel that rests on the floor and has to be notched to fit over the tread is shown in **8-17**. Another approach is to notch the newel as needed, to line it up with the centerline of the balustrade and bolt it to the stringer and skirtboard. Then notch the tread around the newel. This is an easy way to secure the newel but does not produce the highest quality of results (**8-18**).

The layout and cutting of an angle landing newel is much more difficult because you have to fit it over the top tread of the first flight, the landing, and the first tread of the upper flight. An allowance is made to enable the newel to extend down against the landing so that you can secure the newel in place (**8-19**). The actual cuts could vary from this depending upon the situation. The example in **8-20** is not for any particular stair but is used to show the cuts that are typically needed. Some builders get their measurements by placing the newel against the stair and landing and marking each location. As you cut the notches, make trial checks and trim lightly until the newel fits. Another approach to installing an angle newel is shown in **8-21**. The newel is set on the landing and lagged into the stringer. The tread is notched to fit around the newel post.

8-19 The angle newel is often designed to extend down the corner, providing excellent connection surface, and is very decorative.

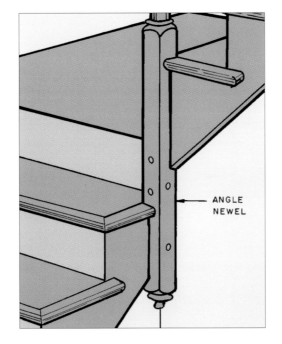

ANGLE NEWEL

8-21 This angle newel post is mounted on the tread and to the stringer.

8-20 An angle newel on a landing is a complex thing to lay out. It has to fit against the risers and treads on two levels as well as the landing. It will vary some, depending upon the design of the stair.

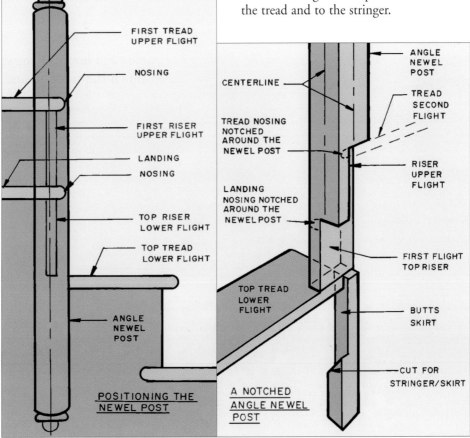

CENTERLINE

FIRST TREAD UPPER FLIGHT

NOSING

FIRST RISER UPPER FLIGHT

LANDING NOSING

TOP RISER LOWER FLIGHT

TOP TREAD LOWER FLIGHT

ANGLE NEWEL POST

POSITIONING THE NEWEL POST

CENTERLINE

TREAD NOSING NOTCHED AROUND THE NEWEL POST

LANDING NOSING NOTCHED AROUND THE NEWEL POST

TOP TREAD LOWER FLIGHT

A NOTCHED ANGLE NEWEL POST

ANGLE NEWEL POST

TREAD SECOND FLIGHT

RISER UPPER FLIGHT

FIRST FLIGHT TOP RISER

BUTTS SKIRT

CUT FOR STRINGER/SKIRT

8-22 An angle newel can be notched at the corner of the landing.

Another attachment is shown in **8-22.** The newel post is notched much like that shown in **8-17.** It has been connected to the landing framing with lag screws from inside the landing so that no holes appear on the exposed surfaces. These newels can also be connected using one of the mechanical connectors discussed in the following pages.

MECHANICAL CONNECTORS

There are a variety of mechanical connectors available for securing the newel post to the floor or to a tread. Following are some that are in general use.

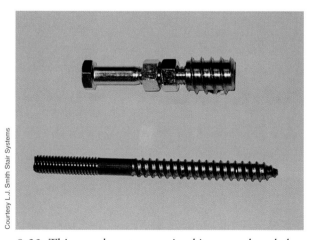

8-23 This newel-post mounting kit uses a threaded insert in the tread and a hanger bolt in the end of the newel post.

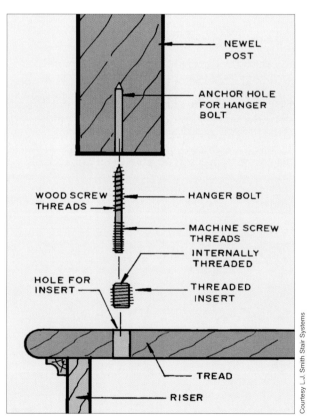

8-24 The threaded insert is screwed into a hole bored in the tread. The hanger bolt is screwed into the bottom of the newel post and then the post is screwed into the treaded insert.

If the newel post rests on the floor or on a tread (refer to **8-9**) you can mount it with an insert and a hanger bolt (**8-23**). Place two-inch blocking between the joists below the floor. Locate the center of the newel post on the floor and bore a hole for the insert. Use the hole diameter recommended with the insert. Bore the hole deeper than the length of the insert so it seats flush with the subfloor (**8-24**). Countersink the hole a little so the edge of the hole does not splinter as the insert is screwed into place.

Screw the insert into the hole using the bolt that came with it. When the insert is flush, unscrew the bolt.

Now install the hanger bolt in the bottom of the newel post. First, cut the post to the desired length so that the handrail is at the required height. Be certain that the cut is square with the side of the post. Draw lines across the diagonals to locate the center. Bore an anchor hole at the center for the wood screw threads on the hanger bolt to screw into. Be very careful to bore the hole perpendicular to the bottom of the post. Screw the bolt into the post, leaving just the part with the machine screw threads sticking out (**8-25**).

Insert the machine screw in the insert and turn the newel until it is tight. Check to be cer-

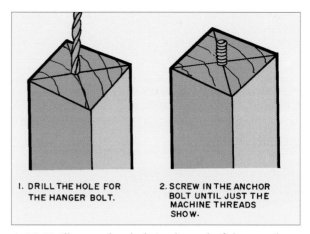

8-25 Drill an anchor hole in the end of the newel and screw in the hanger bolt until only the machine screw is protruding.

tain it is plumb. If necessary, sand or scrape a bit off the bottom until it seats plumb. When this is complete, loosen it and coat the post and floor with glue. Retighten the post and give the glue time to set before you do other work involving it. This connection is not as strong as the newel post bolted to the floor joist or blocking.

If the house has a concrete floor, secure a metal post anchor to the floor, screw the newel to it, and cut a hole in the tread for the post (**8-26**). The newel can be secured to the carriage with lag screws.

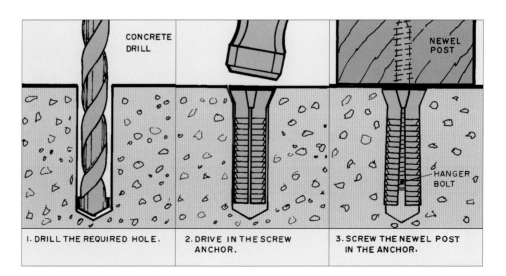

8-26 Screw anchors can be used to secure the newel post to concrete floors.

To provide a strong connection for a free-standing newel post like the one in **8-27**, a newel-fastening system that incorporates an 11-inch hanger bolt is used (**8-28**). It runs through the tread and into solid two-inch-thick bracing installed for this connection. Installation details are shown in **8-29**.

The newel is often mounted to the starting step by mounting a large-diameter dowel in the newel. Holes are drilled through the tread and top block-ing. The dowel is cut so it rests firmly on the top of the second blocking. A lag screw is run through the blocking into the dowel. Glue is applied as the dowel is inserted into the starting step (**8-30**).

After cutting the newel post to the required length to get the handrail the required height, bore a hole for the dowel. Insert the dowel and slide it into the hole in the starting step and make a trial fit. Adjust the length of the dowel until it sits firmly on the lower blocking and the newel sits firmly on the tread. Check it with a square to see that it is plumb. If not, remove small amounts from the bottom of the newel until it is plumb (**8-31**).

Coat the inside of the dowel hole and the dowel and the bottom of the newel with epoxy adhesive. Slide the post on

8-27 This freestanding newel post needs an extra strong con-nection because it is not supported by other parts of the balustrade and is positioned where it could frequently be bumped.

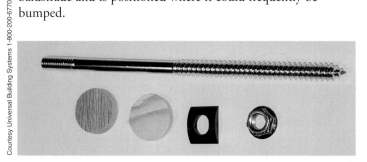

8-28 This newel-post connector uses a long hanger bolt to secure the newel to the stair framing.

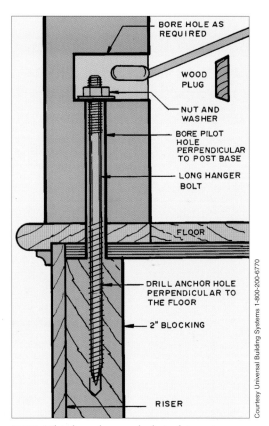

BORE HOLE AS REQUIRED

WOOD PLUG

NUT AND WASHER

BORE PILOT HOLE PERPENDICULAR TO POST BASE

LONG HANGER BOLT

FLOOR

DRILL ANCHOR HOLE PERPENDICULAR TO THE FLOOR

2" BLOCKING

RISER

8-29 This long hanger bolt is driven into the blocking set behind the riser. It provides a strong newel-post connection.

8-30 Starting newels can be secured to the starting step with a large-diameter wood dowel.

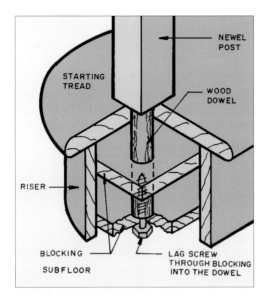

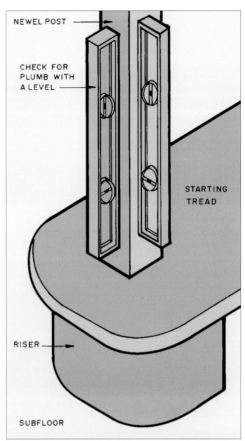

the dowel and press it firmly in place. Install the lag screw, pulling the newel post tight. Check it for plumb.

A post fastener using metal L-brackets to secure the post to the floor is shown in **8-32**. The post is secured with the brackets and the mitered oak trim is installed covering them (**8-33**).

8-31 Glue the dowel into the holes in the tread and blocking and check for plumb. Consider bracing it to the floor with 1 × 2 wood pieces nailed to the floor and clamped to the newel post to hold it plumb as the glue dries.

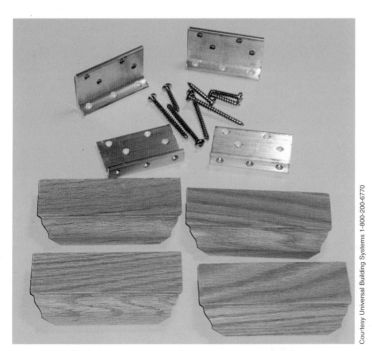

8-32 This kit lets you connect the newel post to the floor or to a tread with metal angles, and provides a wood base to cover them.

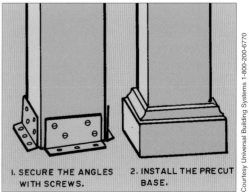

8-33 Secure the metal angles to the newel and floor with the screws provided. Then nail the premitered base around the newel.

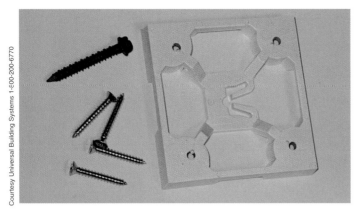

8-34 This plastic post-mounting plate is typically used to secure porch posts that are braced with a strong railing.

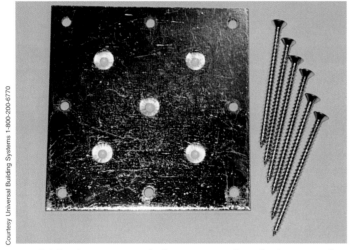

8-36 This kit uses a steel plate connected to the bottom of the newel post and screwed to the floor. The plate is then covered with a molding.

Another post mount uses a plastic base that is screwed to the bottom of the post (**8-34**). An anchor screw is set into the floor. The post is slid on the screw and it snaps into place (**8-35**). A newel post fastener is shown in **8-36**. It is screwed to

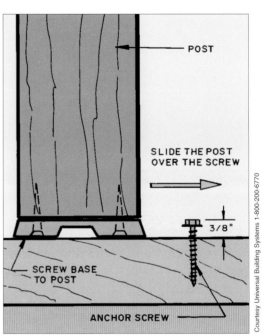

POST

SLIDE THE POST OVER THE SCREW

3/8"

SCREW BASE TO POST

ANCHOR SCREW

8-35 Secure the plastic base to the bottom of the post. Mount the anchor screw at the location for the center of the post. Slide the post with the notch in the base, facing the screw over the screw until it snaps in place.

8-37 This newel-post mounting plate will let you set the post centered on it or shifted to one edge. After the post is anchored with the connector as seen in 8-36, you can conceal it with standard base and quarter round.

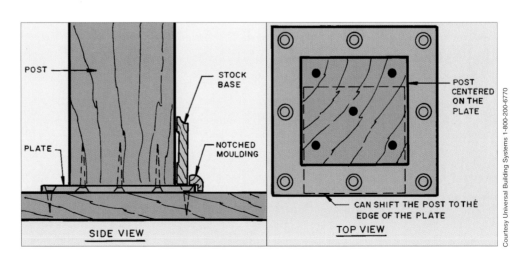

POST

PLATE

STOCK BASE

NOTCHED MOULDING

SIDE VIEW

POST CENTERED ON THE PLATE

CAN SHIFT THE POST TO THE EDGE OF THE PLATE

TOP VIEW

the post and then to the floor or tread. A molding and quarter round can be placed around it, as shown in **8-37**.

Newel posts are available in a wide variety of designs. Those for post-to-post connections will have a turned decorative finial on the top. Those used for over-the-post balustrades will have a dowel on top to connect to a fitting (**8-38**).

THE BALUSTRADE

The balustrade is made up of a handrail, balusters, and various fittings. **Handrails** are manufactured in a number of different profiles. They are available with a flat bottom or a rectangular groove called a plow cut in the bottom as seen in the left example in **8-39**. This bottom plow is used to set the balusters on top of some balustrade designs.

Balusters are also available in a wide range of designs. Many of the styles are copies of those that were used in early American homes. The style shown in **8-40** has a round top whereas other designs will have a square section on the top. Some styles are fluted and have extensive turnings.

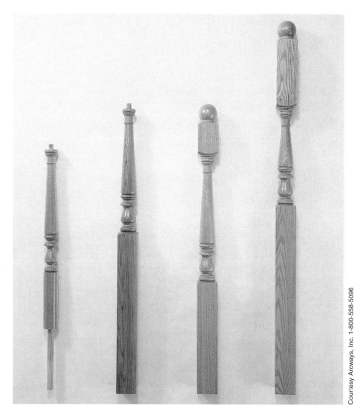

8-38 A series of newel posts designed for over-the-post and post-to-post balustrades.

Courtesy Arcways, Inc. 1-800-558-5096

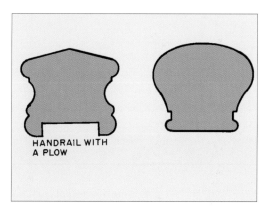

HANDRAIL WITH A PLOW

8-39 These are just two of the many handrail profiles available.

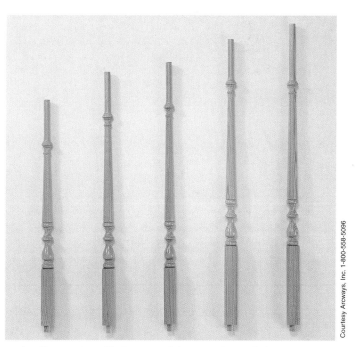

Courtesy Arcways, Inc. 1-800-558-5096

8-40 One series of balusters of the Neoclassical design.

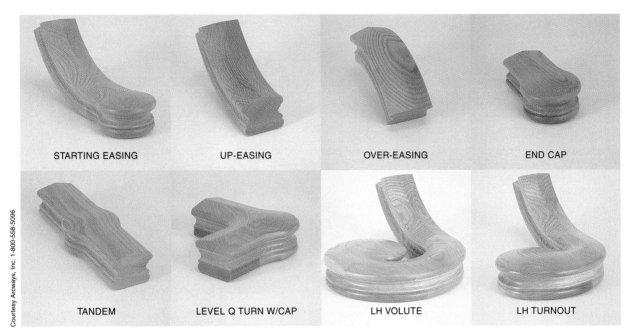

Courtesy Arcways, Inc. 1-800-558-5096

STARTING EASING

UP-EASING

OVER-EASING

END CAP

TANDEM

LEVEL Q TURN W/CAP

LH VOLUTE

LH TURNOUT

8-41 Typical fittings manufactured for over-the-post balustrades.

The handrail for over-the-post is connected to the newel post with **fittings**. They are available in profiles to match the handrail. There are fittings that run the handrail straight across a newel post or that turn the handrail left or right. Some are curved, connecting the handrail to the starting newel post (**8-41**). **Goosenecks** are used to lower the handrail from a floor or landing down to the height of the handrail on the stair below. Examples are in **8-42**. Some goosenecks turn the handrail 90 degrees and do not require a newel post at the corner.

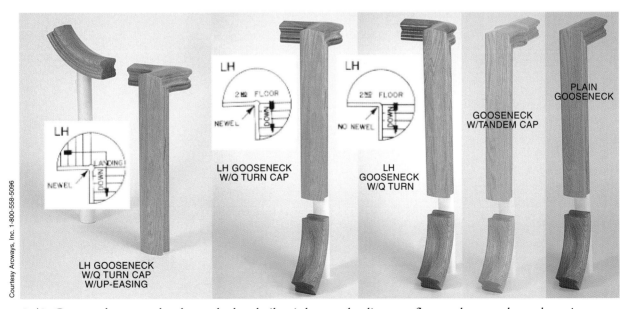

Courtesy Arcways, Inc. 1-800-558-5096

LH GOOSENECK
W/Q TURN CAP
W/UP-EASING

LH GOOSENECK
W/Q TURN CAP

LH
GOOSENECK
W/Q TURN

GOOSENECK
W/TANDEM CAP

PLAIN
GOOSENECK

8-42 Goosenecks are used to lower the handrail as it leaves a landing or a floor and moves down the stair.

CONSTRUCTING STAIRCASES, BALUSTRADES & LANDINGS

INSTALLING
A POST-TO-POST
BALUSTRADE

The process varies depending upon the techniques of the stair builder, but the following is typical.

1. Locate the balusters on the treads. They will be located on the centerline of the handrail and spaced evenly along the balustrade. Remember that some codes limit the space between them to 4 inches and others 6 inches. Your stair must confrom to your local code. The first baluster generally is placed so it lines up with the face of the riser.

Make a sample sketch of the stair and the size of the balustrade you plan to use. Compare this to your local code; it will show whether your plan meets the code (**8-43**).

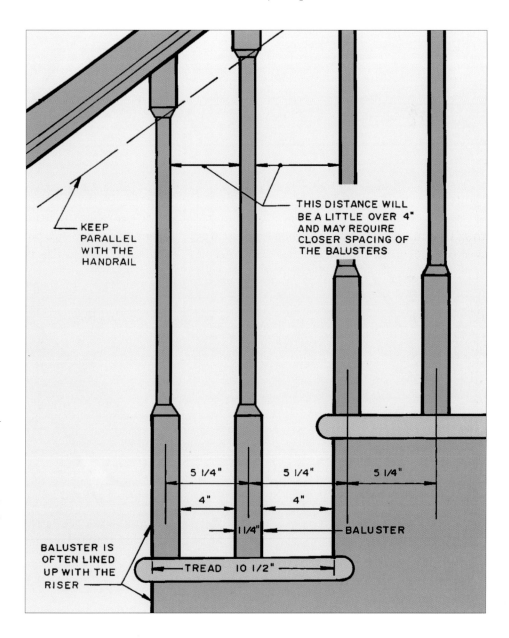

8-43 Make a drawing of the stair, locate the handrail, and space the balusters. The spacing will vary depending upon the size of the tread, balusters, and the local building code. Some situations may require three balusters per tread.

KEEP PARALLEL WITH THE HANDRAIL

THIS DISTANCE WILL BE A LITTLE OVER 4" AND MAY REQUIRE CLOSER SPACING OF THE BALUSTERS

5 1/4" 5 1/4" 5 1/4"

4" 4"

1 1/4" BALUSTER

BALUSTER IS OFTEN LINED UP WITH THE RISER

TREAD 10 1/2"

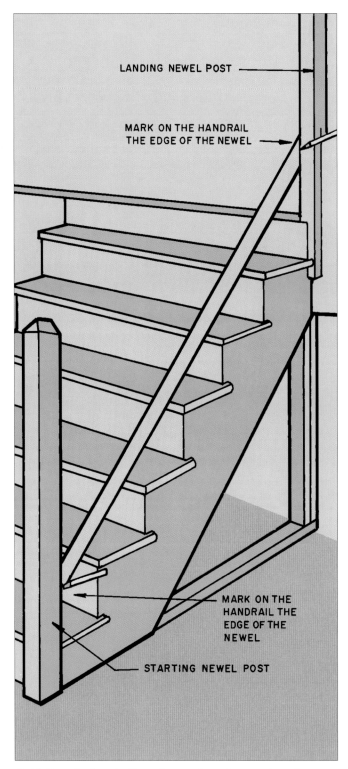

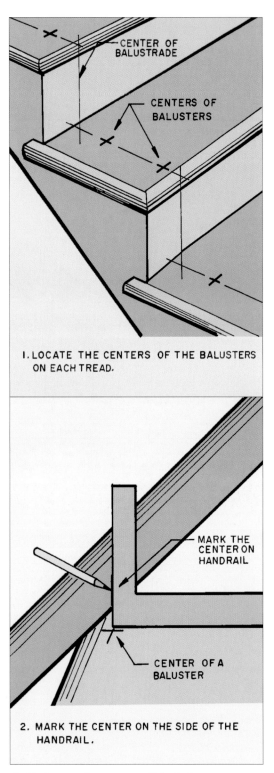

8-44 Lay the handrail on the treads and up against the newel posts. Mark the location of the edge of the newel post on the handrail.

8-45 Locate the centers of the balusters on each tread. Use a square to transfer the centers of the balusters to the side of the handrail.

2. Lay the handrail along the top of the treads and against the newel posts. You can mark the length by scribing along each newel post (**8-44**). With a square, you can transfer the baluster locations from the top of the tread to the handrail (**8-45**). It helps if you clamp the handrail as you mark it. Otherwise it tends to slip.

3. Locate the centers for the holes for the balusters on the bottom of the handrail (**8-46**).

4. If the baluster has a dowel on the end, bore holes in the treads for them. Be certain that the holes are perpendicular to the tread and a little deeper than the length of the dowel.

   Another technique is to use dowel screws (**8-47**). The kit includes several dowel screws and a driver that lets you install them with your electric drill, as shown in **8-48**.

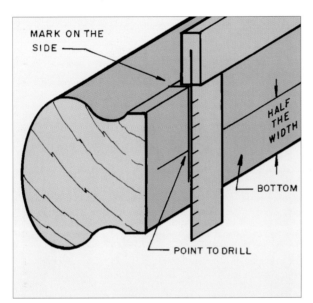

8-46 Move the mark to the centerline of the handrail to locate the center of the hole to be drilled for the baluster.

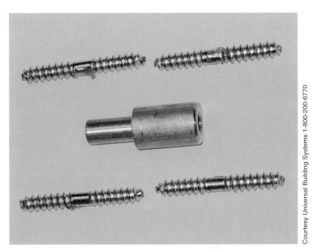

Courtesy Universal Building Systems 1-800-200-6770

8-47 Dowel screws in this kit are used to secure the balusters to the treads. A special driver is supplied so that you can use your electric drill to drive the screws.

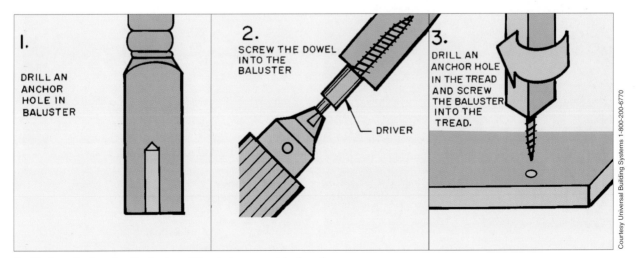

Courtesy Universal Building Systems 1-800-200-6770

8-48 Installation details for installing balusters with dowel screws.

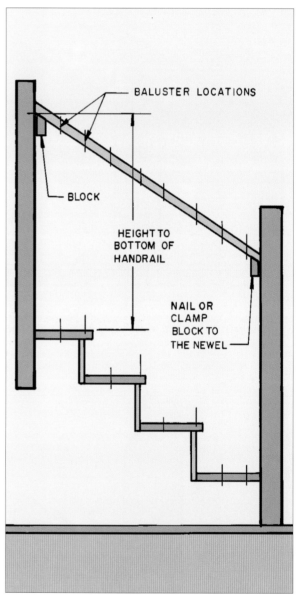

You can also connect balusters to the treads using a hanger bolt and threaded inserts, as described for newel post installation in **8-23** and **8-24**, on pages 108 and 109.

You can find the center of the balustrade by crossing the diagonals or by using the hole center in **8-49**.

BALUSTER LOCATIONS

BLOCK

HEIGHT TO BOTTOM OF HANDRAIL

NAIL OR CLAMP BLOCK TO THE NEWEL

⅜" ELECTRIC DRILL

CENTAUR™

BALUSTER BASE

8-49 This tool is placed over the end of the baluster and centers the drill on it.

8-50 Temporarily hold the handrail at the desired height by clamping it to blocks secured to the newel post.

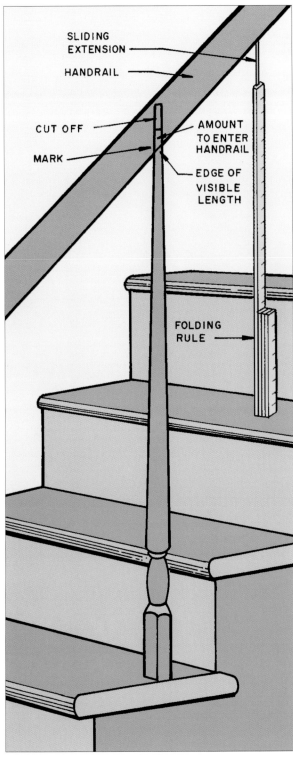

8-51 Measure to find the length of the exposed part of the baluster, and add the required amount to fit into the handrail.

5. Measure up each newel post to the height of the bottom of the handrail. Tack or clamp blocks of scrap wood here and rest the handrail on them (8-50). You could hold the blocks with clamps if you do not want a hole in the newel post.

6. Place a baluster in the dowel hole in the tread or flat on the tread if a dowel screw is to be used. When you are certain it is perpendicular, mark the length wanted at the handrail. Allow about ¾ inch to extend into the bottom of the handrail. The diameter of the baluster at the bottom of the handrail is the diameter of the hole you will bore into the bottom (8-51). Cut the balusters to length.

Typically the balusters are cut with the square section on the tread the same length (8-52).

8-52 Typically the square end of the balustrades are cut the same length on all the balusters.

A more interesting technique is to step the balusters by shortening the length of the square section on the tread, starting with the first one as shown in **8-53**. The amount removed should keep the edges on the same slope as the stair. When you use this method, the hole in the bottom of the handrail will most likely have a smaller diameter than the one for the next baluster because the taper in the top narrows toward the end.

Another technique is to measure the distance from the tread to the bottom of the handrail. You can use a folding rule with a square end that has an extension (**8-51**); make your own sliding rule or use the telescoping baluster marking tool in **8-54**. Remember to allow extra length to go into the hole in the handrail.

Courtesy Arcways, Inc. 1-800-558-5096

8-53 An attractive way to install the balusters is to step the length of the square end. Keep the tops of the square sections parallel with the slope of the stair.

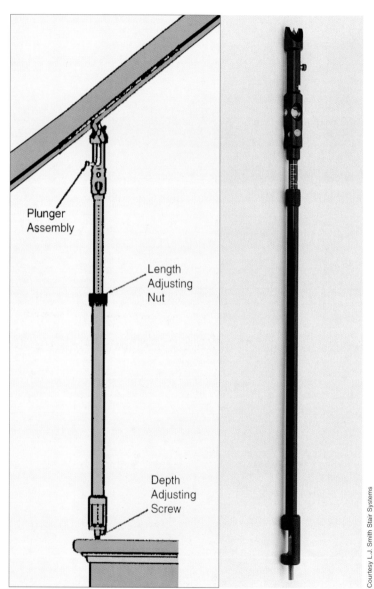

Plunger Assembly

Length Adjusting Nut

Depth Adjusting Screw

Courtesy L.J. Smith Stair Systems

8-54 This is a telescoping baluster-marking tool used to measure baluster length. It is also used to locate the hole in the bottom of the handrail by setting it on the mark on the tread and adjusting until it is plumb.

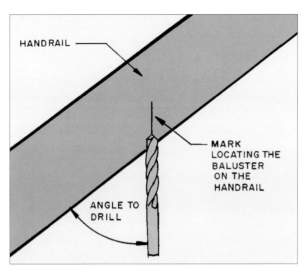

8-55 The hole in the bottom of the handrail is drilled using the angle made by the original mark used to locate the baluster.

7. Bore the holes in the bottom of the handrail. They must be on the angle produced when you marked the location of each baluster (8-55). A stair installer will use a special tool that clamps to the handrail and is adjusted to the correct angle. The bit is guided by the tool so the hole is accurately bored (8-56). Bore the hole deep enough so the end of the baluster will not touch the bottom. The manufacturer provides detailed instructions for mounting and adjusting the tool.

8. Now make a dry assembly of the balustrade to be certain everything fits properly and no dowels are so large that they will not fit in the dowel holes. Check for plumb and for ascertaining that the assembly is straight.

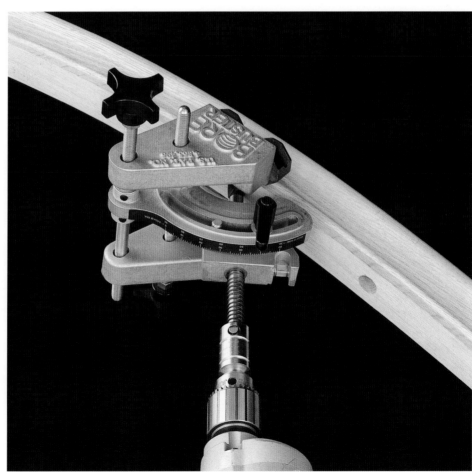

8-56 This tool, called Bore Buster®, is adjustable to permit accurate boring of holes for balusters in the handrail. It also permits accurate boring of holes for connectors in the ends of handrails.

Courtesy L.J. Smith Stairway Systems

8-57 This handrail installation kit provides a connection between the newel post and handrail in post-to-post balustrades.

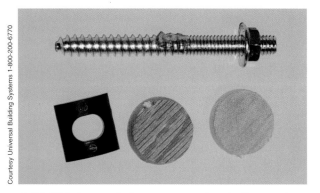

8-59 This hanger-bolt can connect handrails, newels, and handrails to walls and is completely hidden.

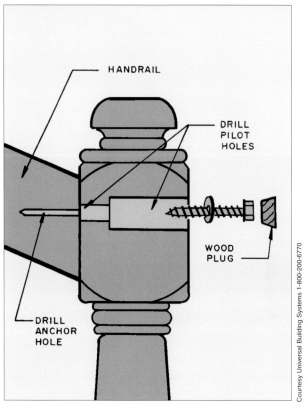

HANDRAIL

DRILL PILOT HOLES

WOOD PLUG

DRILL ANCHOR HOLE

8-58 Drill pilot and anchor holes as specified by the manufacturer. Install with a socket wrench. Then glue the wood plug in place and sand smooth after the glue has dried.

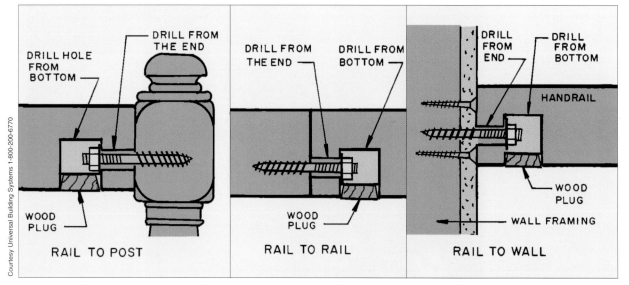

DRILL HOLE FROM BOTTOM

DRILL FROM THE END

WOOD PLUG

RAIL TO POST

DRILL FROM THE END

DRILL FROM BOTTOM

WOOD PLUG

RAIL TO RAIL

DRILL FROM END

DRILL FROM BOTTOM

HANDRAIL

WOOD PLUG

WALL FRAMING

RAIL TO WALL

8-60 Install this connector by drilling a hole in the end of the handrail and in the bottom. Tighten the hanger bolt in the end of the handrail. Slide the end with machine threads in the hole and tighten the nut.

9. Now you are ready to assemble the balustrade. First, you should decide how you will connect the handrail to the newel posts. If you decide that they will be connected with a hanger bolt or lag screw, you will have to prepare the handrail before installing the balusters. A kit providing a lag screw, washer, and wood plugs is shown in **8-57**. Installation details can be seen in **8-58**. Measure the depth of the holes carefully when you are drilling the pilot holes so that the threads will penetrate the handrail enough to get a strong connection.

Another handrail connector uses a hanger bolt. The kit contains everything needed (**8-59**). It has the advantage of being completely hidden from view. Look at the installation detail in **8-60**. The handrail has a pilot hole drilled from the end and a hole in the bottom so the nut can be put on the end of the machine screw. This connector also has use on rail-to-rail connections and is used to secure the end of the handrail to a wall. The hanger bolt is installed with a special wrench, which is also used to install and tighten the nut as shown in **8-61** and **8-62**.

8-61 This special rail bolt wrench is used to screw the hanger bolt into the end of the handrail and to thread the nut onto hanger bolts inside the handrail and tighten them against the washer.

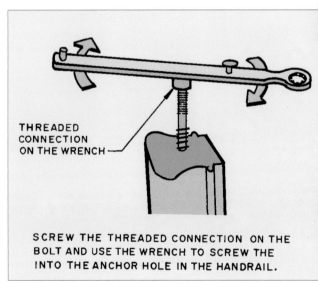

THREADED CONNECTION ON THE WRENCH —

SCREW THE THREADED CONNECTION ON THE BOLT AND USE THE WRENCH TO SCREW THE INTO THE ANCHOR HOLE IN THE HANDRAIL.

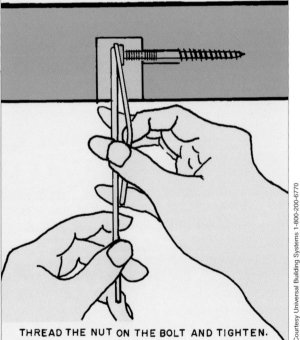

THREAD THE NUT ON THE BOLT AND TIGHTEN.

8-62 How to use the special wrench to install the concealed connector.

A simple angle connector kit is shown in **8-63.** While it is easy to use, it is visible after installation (**8-64**).

If the handrail is to butt a finished wall, it is secured to a rosette that is nailed through the wallboard into a stud. The handrail is secured to the rosette with wood screws.

10. Take the balustrade apart and glue the baluster dowels to the treads. Place glue on the top of the balusters and a little on the dowels and in the dowel holes, and fit them into the dowel holes in the handrail. Be certain the balusters are set so the square bottom section is parallel with the end of the tread. You can tap on the handrail if necessary, to assure the balusters are firmly seated. Use a wood block covered with carpet so you do not

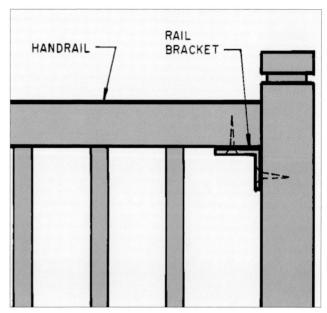

8-64 Secure the bracket below the handrail to the post. The angle bracket provides a connection fro the handrail to the post, but it is still visible after installation.

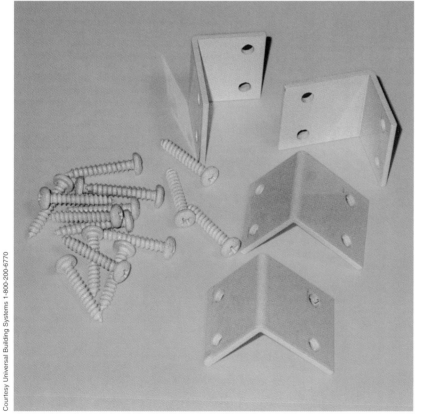

8-63 This heavily coated bracket is used to secure the handrail to the post.

damage the handrail. Some balusters are square on the top and bottom. They are installed on handrails that have a groove plowed on the bottom to receive them.

To establish its length, place the baluster on a tread and place this against the handrail. Mark the angle of the handrail on the baluster (8-65). Allow an additional amount so it fits snuggly into the plow. After you cut one, try it to be certain it is the right length. Then cut the others the same size.

Install the baluster by placing it on the tread and against the handrail. Check for plumb, then drill small holes for the nails that are used to toe-nail it to the handrail. After all are in place, cut and nail filler blocks between them (8-66).

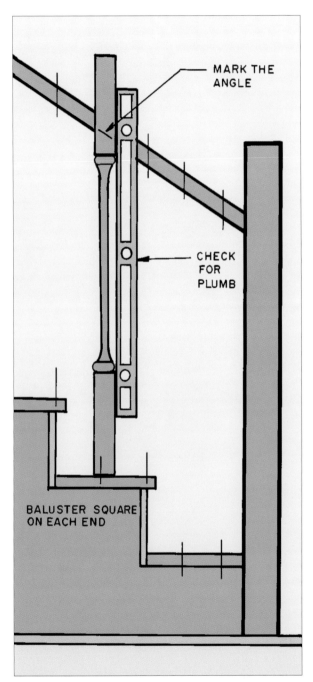

8-65 Balusters that are square on both ends have the top end cut on the same angle as the handrail.

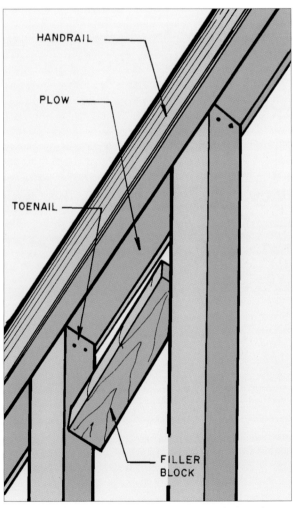

8-66 The square-end balustrade is toenailed to the bottom of the handrail and filler blocks are nailed in between, in the plow.

8-67 A post-to-post stairway built using stock lumber and nailed connections forming the balustrade.

A SIMPLE VARIATION

Post-to-post construction is often used to build a stair with simple connections that incoorporates basically stock lumber. A post-to-post stair is shown in **8-67**. The treads and the deck of the landing are made using kiln-dried lumber that has been dressed to 1- or 1¼-inch thickness (**8-68**). The balustrade uses stock 2 × 4 material for the handrail. The edges have been rounded with a router. The balusters have been made with stock 2 × 2 material (**8-69**). When the assembled stair has been stained and finished with a protective clear coating, it is an attractive and inexpensive stairway.

8-68 The treads and decking are stock construction materials. Be certain they are kiln dried.

8-69 The handrail is made using kiln-dried 2 × 4 and 2 × 2 construction lumber.

8-70 This balustrade was made using high-quality oak. The handrails are connected to the newel posts with standard metal connectors.

8-71 The oak balusters are secured to the side of the wide handrail and the side of the stairwell opening and stringer.

A different approach to the use of kiln-dried lumber was made in the balustrade in **8-70**. The entire construction was made using high-quality kiln-dried oak. The large handrail has the top corners machined round. The balusters are 2 × 2 oak and are fastened to the side of the handrail and the edge of stairwell and stringer (**8-71**).

INSTALLING AN OVER-THE-POST BALUSTRADE

An over-the-post balustrade is more difficult to install than the post-to-post type. The best way to learn how to do this is to work with an experienced stair installer. Each has methods developed over the years of producing quality stairs. The measuring, cutting, fitting and assembly require the highest level of technical competence.

There are available a number of tools developed that provide a great deal of assistance in assembling and installing the rail fittings. These will be shown as the assembly proceeds. Refer to **8-41** and **8-42**, on page 114, for information on fittings and goosenecks.

Stair builders begin by accurately determining the height of the newel posts and then the location and lengths of the fittings, and finally the length of the handrail. To do this some builders prepare a full-sized drawing of the stair at each newel post and lay out the fittings on the drawing. Using the actual fittings as the templates.

You begin by making a full-sized drawing of the treads and risers associated with the newel post and then locate the centerline of the newel post in relation to these. The post can be located in several positions in relation to the first step. Refer back to situations described earlier in this chapter. The drawing need not be the full length of the stair but show several treads at each newel post (**8-72**).

Many stair builders use a pitch block to locate and mark the cuts required on the fittings and handrail. A pitch block is a triangular pattern with sides equal to the rise and run of the stair (**8-73**).

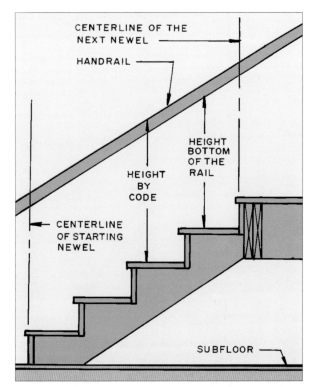

8-72 Prepare a full-sized drawing showing the newels on each end. You need not draw all of the treads but just enough to get the basic layout. The length of the handrail on this shortened drawing is not true length.

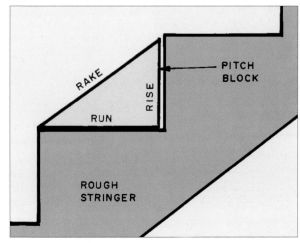

8-73 A pitch block is made using the rise and run of the stair.

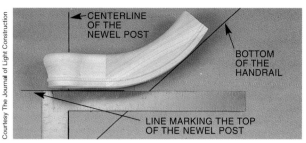

CENTERLINE
OF THE
NEWEL POST

BOTTOM
OF THE
HANDRAIL

LINE MARKING THE TOP
OF THE NEWEL POST

8-74 The height of the starting newel is found by centering the dowel hole in the starting, easing over the centerline of the newel on the drawing. Place a straightedge perpendicular to the centerline and just touching the easing. Slide the easing down until the bottom surface touches the straightedge. Draw a line at this point to locate the newel post's height.

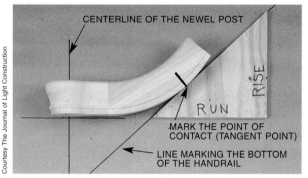

CENTERLINE OF THE NEWEL POST

RISE

RUN

MARK THE POINT OF
CONTACT (TANGENT POINT)

LINE MARKING THE BOTTOM
OF THE HANDRAIL

8-75 To find the point at which to cut the easing where it butts the handrail, place the pitch block with the run side on the horizontal line. Slide it until it makes contact. Mark this is point (the tangent point).

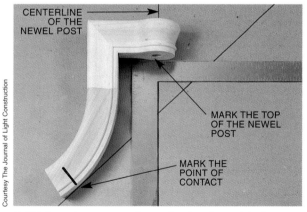

CENTERLINE
OF THE
NEWEL POST

MARK THE TOP
OF THE NEWEL
POST

MARK THE
POINT OF
CONTACT

8-77 Lay the gooseneck on the drawing with the dowel hole lined up with the newel centerline and the curved end touching the line representing the bottom of the handrail.

First, locate the height of the newel post on the drawing. Do this by laying the fitting to be on top of the newel post on the drawing. Line up the centerline of the dowel hole in it with the centerline of the newel post. Mark where the bottom of the fitting crosses the centerline of the newel post (8-74).

Now locate the point at which the fitting and handrail will join end-to-end (8-75). Carefully slide up against the bottom of the fitting, keeping it in perfect alignment with the line representing the bottom of the handrail. Mark the point where they touch. This is the location for cutting the fitting to length.

To lay out the angle of cut on the fitting, turn the pitch block as shown in 8-76. Place the riser side horizontally on the line of the top of the newel post and mark along the rake side of the pitch block. Cut on this line. The handrail is cut square on the end and joins the fitting at this cut.

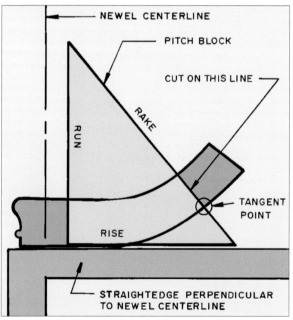

NEWEL CENTERLINE

PITCH BLOCK

CUT ON THIS LINE

RAKE

RUN

RISE

TANGENT
POINT

STRAIGHTEDGE PERPENDICULAR
TO NEWEL CENTERLINE

8-76 To mark the angle of the cut, place the pitch block with the rise on the horizontal line. Slide it until the rake touches the tangent point. Draw a line along the rake to locate the cutting line.

Repeat the process for the newel post at the top of the stair (8-77). Place the gooseneck fitting on the drawing and slide it down so the curved bottom touches the line representing the bottom of the handrail. Be certain the centerline of the dowel hole in the fitting is in perfect alignment with the centerline of the newel post (8-78). Mark the top of the newel post. Use a pitch block to locate the point of intersection between the fitting and the handrail. The fittings are cut on this mark perpendicular to the line representing the end of the handrail. The installation in 8-79 shows how the gooseneck turns the corner and lowers the handrail to the height needed to meet the fitting on the next newel post. A finished gooseneck installation is seen in 8-80. Notice that the joint between the gooseneck and handrail was so carefully made it is not noticeable.

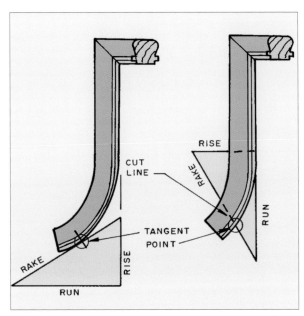

8-78 Locate the tangent point on the curve with the pitch block, with the run side on the horizontal. Then place the run side on the vertical side of the lower piece and mark the angle of cut along the rake side.

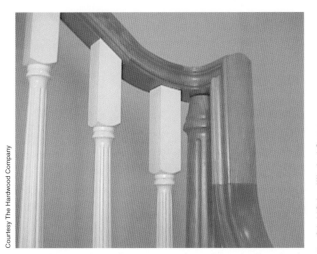

8-79 Notice how this gooseneck enables the handrail to turn a corner and lowers it to the height of the handrail on the flight below.

8-80 A finished handrail showing the gooseneck and handrail connections.

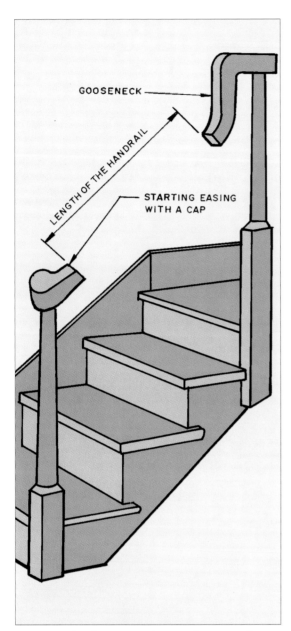

8-82 Tighten the handrail to the fitting using the special wrench available from the connector manufacturer.

8-81 Set the fittings on the newel posts and carefully measure the length of the handrail needed. This requires careful work. Measure several times to verify the distance.

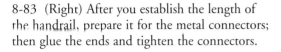

8-83 (Right) After you establish the length of the handrail, prepare it for the metal connectors; then glue the ends and tighten the connectors.

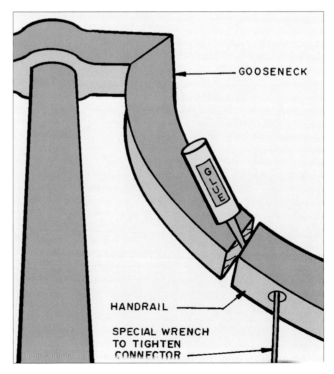

Now you know the length of the newel posts, so cut them to size and secure in place. Several methods are suggested earlier in this chapter.

Cut the fittings on the mark. Use a fine-toothed power saw such as a miter saw. Set the fittings on the dowel pins on top of the newel posts and measure the distance between them to find the length of the handrail. This is a very crucial measurement. If it is a bit long, you can shave off a bit with the miter saw. Usually just a fine shaving of sawdust is trimmed. If it is too short, you have a problem (**8-81**).

Secure the handrail to the fittings using handrail bolts. This is a tedious process that requires careful work and often many adjustments to get a perfect tight end joint. Methods for making this connection are shown earlier in this chapter.

Fit the handrail over the bolt, get the nut on the bolt, and then pull the parts together by tightening the nut (**8-82**). Check to be certain that thee joint closes completely. Then loosen the nut and coat the ends with a polyvinyl or aliphatic resin (**8-83**).

Mark the location of each baluster on the tread and on the bottom of the handrail. On some types of fittings balustrades will be inserted in them. Then assemble the balustrade as described earlier in this chapter, pages 115 to 125. A finished over-the-post ballustrade installation is shown in **8-84**.

8-84 This L-shaped stair uses turnout fittings on the starting newel and quarter-turn goosenecks with up-easing and a cap.

INSTALLING THE BALUSTRADE

A finished balustrade with a volute on the starting newel is seen in **8-85**. The layout is basically the same as described, but notice that the volute extends well beyond the newel post and is supported by a number of balusters. The volute installation in **8-86** shows how the balusters are laid out along the volute.

In addition to wood balusters, a number of wrought-iron systems are available, such as the one shown in **8-87**. This construction of wood for the handrails and newel posts and wrought iron for the balusters serves as the stair and landing balustrade.

8-86 A volute on the starting newel provides an unusual and striking beginning on the handrail.

8-85 This stair uses a starting step to support a volute and several balusters installed in the volute. The volute is joined to the newel post.

8-87 Wrought-iron balusters provide a delicate decorative balustrade.

Various accessories are available to enhance the stair and provide a finished, quality appearance. These include items such as a tread bracket, rosette, and various finials. The tread bracket is used on the skirt below the tread (**8-88**). The rosette is used to terminate a handrail at a wall (**8-89**). The finial is used atop a newel post to give a decorative finish (**8-90**).

8-88 A tread bracket is installed on the stringer below the tread. It covers any crack at the tread and provides a decorative feature.

8-89 A rosette is secured to the end of the handrail, enabling it to terminate against a gypsum wallboard or plaster wall.

8-90 A finial on the newel gives a finished appearance.

Courtesy Journal of Light Construction

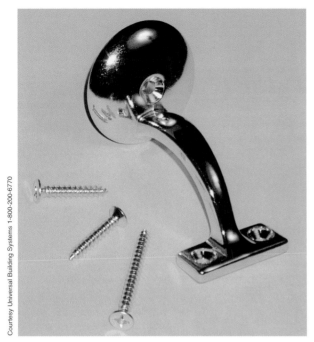

8-91 This bracket is screwed to blocking behind the wallboard and carries the handrail down a closed wall.

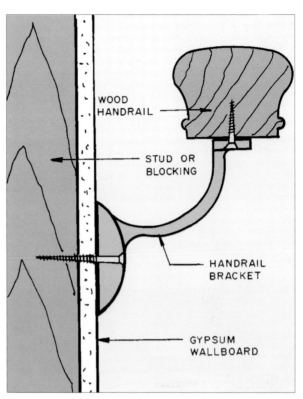

WOOD HANDRAIL

STUD OR BLOCKING

HANDRAIL BRACKET

GYPSUM WALLBOARD

8-92 This bracket holds the handrail to the wall and provides the spacing required by the building code.

HANDRAILS FOR CLOSED STAIRS

Handrails for closed stairs are generally mounted on the wall with metal handrail brackets, as shown in **8-91**. The bracket is designed so that when a stock handrail is mounted there will be at least 1½ inches clear space between it and the wall. The brackets can be mounted on wall studs. However, blocking between studs is frequently used (**8-92**).

CHAPTER 9

Open-Riser Stairs

9-1 This manufactured open-riser stairway does not block the view. As a result the room is lighter and seems larger.

Courtesy Designed Stairs, Inc. 1-877-4Stairs

Open-riser stairs enable the homeowners and their guests to see through them. When used within a room they make the room seem larger. They are also an attractive architectural feature. Open-riser stairs may be built on-site or ordered from stair manufacturers (9-1).

DESIGNING THE STAIR

The stringer is designed using the same code requirements for closed stair construction when the open-riser stair is used in residential construction, except that some codes require that the vertical distance between treads should not exceed four inches, Check your local codes.

The treads should be thick enough to provide a firm support and not be bouncy. A typical 36-inch-wide stair would generally use a 1¼-inch-thick tread, though some builders use thicker material aesthetically to provide a more substantial and massive appearance.

The stringers can be 2 × 10 or 2 × 12 stock. The treads are usually set in a through or stopped mortise (9-2) with partial or full tenons (9-3). The mortise is cut at least ½ inch deep. The tread is secured in the mortise with glue and screws. This is similar to the housed stringer construction.

9-2 One type of open-riser stair uses a through mortise that receives a square end tread. The stopped mortise is used with either the partial or full tenon on the end of the tread. The size of the mortise depends upon the size of the tenon.

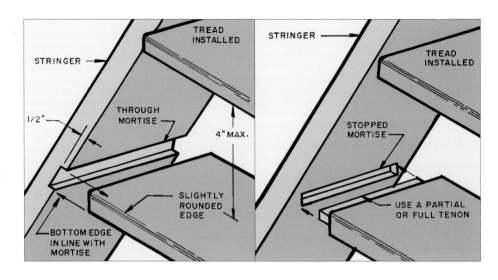

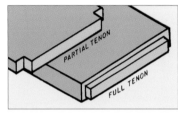

9-3 The partial and full tenons.

The tread can be made from stock 1¼-inch-thick or thicker. It will be 11 inches wide to meet codes. Give the nosing a slight round with your router, but not over a ½ inch radius.

LAYING OUT THE STRINGER

The stringer is laid out by setting a layout line a desired distance below the front of the stringer; you can lay out the treads and risers as described for notched stairs in Chapter 4. These lines locate the bottom of the tread (9-4). Some builders make the actual tread ½ to 1 inch wider so that it extends a little beyond, to the edge of the stringer.

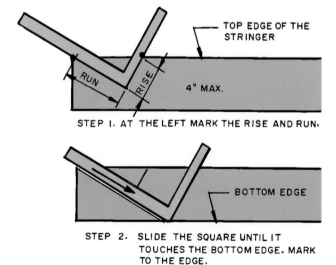

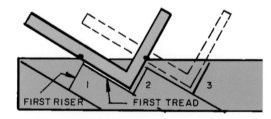

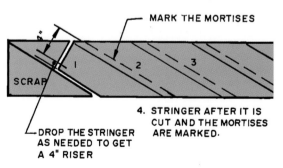

9-4 One way to lay out the stringer for an open-riser stair. Note that some codes limit the riser distance to 4 inches. Check your local code.

CUTTING
THE STRINGER
& TREADS

Probably the easiest way to cut the mortise in the stringer is with a router. This procedure is shown in Chapter 5 on page 65 in **5-15** and **5-16**. If you use a through mortise, cut from each end toward the center. If you cut from the center outward, you may split off the edge when you complete the cut. The stopped mortise is a cut that is usually made with a plunge router. Insert it down into the wood at one end and cut to the other end of the mortise. You will have to square up the corners with a chisel because the router cutter will leave them round (**9-5**). When you lay out the stop mortise, remember to leave an uncut area at each end so the tread can be notched to provide a neat connection. In both cases it helps if you prepare a jig to guide the router as discussed in Chapter 5.

When you cut the treads to length, remember to allow for the length of the mortise. If you are using a stop mortise, cut the tenon on the end of the tread $1/32$ inch short of the depth of the mortise. This allows the front edge of the tread to fit tightly against the stringer and allows a small space for the glue (**9-6**).

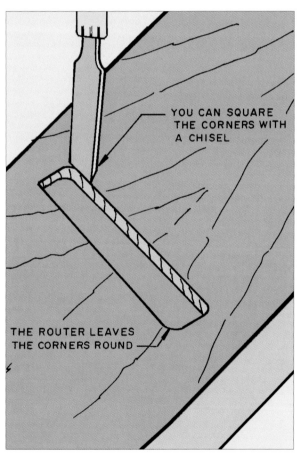

9-5 You can square up the rounded corners of the stopped mortise to fit the corners of the tread. If the tread edges are slightly rounded, they may fit against the rounded corners with little adjustment.

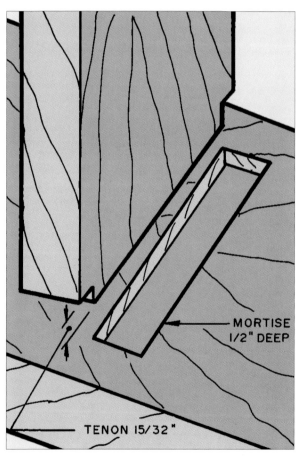

9-6 Cut the tenon a little shorter than the depth of the stopped mortise.

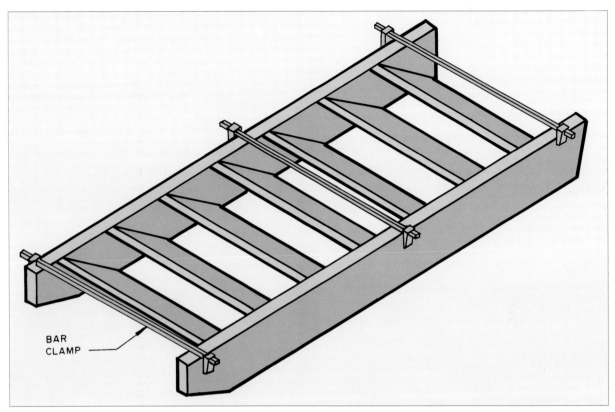

BAR
CLAMP

9-7 Make a trial assembly of the stair before gluing and screwing through the stringers into the treads.

ASSEMBLING
THE STAIR

When using a through mortise, allow the tread nosing to extend far enough at the front to cover the end of the mortise (**9-2**).

It is easiest to assemble the stair on the floor (**9-7**). Install the top and bottom tread. Measure the diagonals to be certain the unit is square (refer to Chapter 5). Then install the remaining treads. Use glue and two 2½-inch wood screws on each end of the treads. Drill pilot holes through the stringer and anchor holes in the end of the tread (**9-8**). It helps if you have some long cabinet clamps to hold the assembly together as you work.

Consider assembling the stair dry, to check to see that each tread fits tightly into the mortise. Usually some slight adjustment is needed. Use a wood chisel to enlarge the mortise as needed; then apply the adhesive and screws.

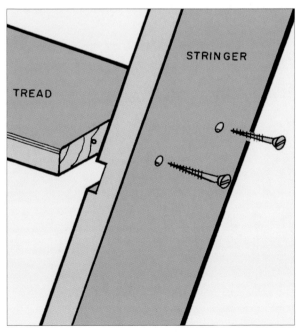

STRINGER

TREAD

9-8 Secure the treads to the stringers with glue and screws.

INSTALLING
THE ASSEMBLED STAIR

The assembled unit is quite heavy and you will need help lifting it into place. Nail a 2 × 4 to the floor where the bottom will rest in order to keep it from sliding as you secure it to the second floor (as described in Chapter 4), or you can use metal connectors here and at the floor (**9-9**).

Open-riser stairs can be used on straight flights and on L-shaped and U-shaped stairs, as described in Chapter 6. See also **9-10**.

MANUFACTURED OPEN-RISER STAIRS

Several stair manufacturers produce attractive and exciting open-riser stairs. One of these is shown in **9-10**. This design rests the treads on wood blocks secured to the massive wood stringers. The thick treads are secured to these blocks and overhang the risers, adding to the attractiveness of the flight. These photos show the open-risers used on a U-shaped stair.

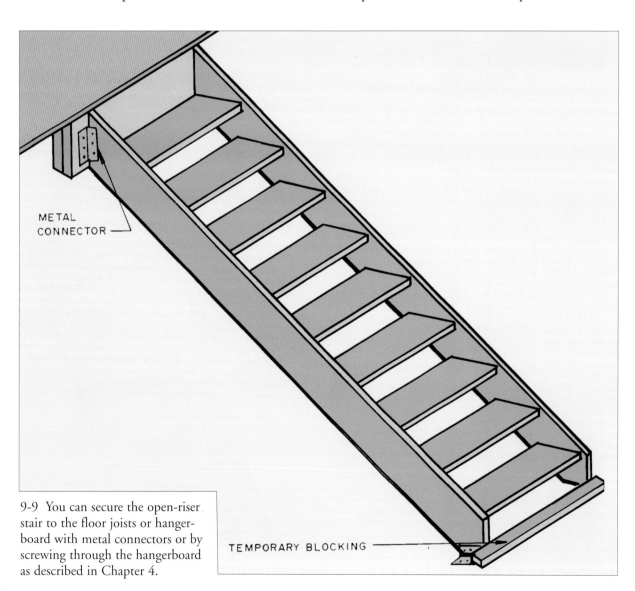

METAL CONNECTOR —

TEMPORARY BLOCKING —

9-9 You can secure the open-riser stair to the floor joists or hanger-board with metal connectors or by screwing through the hangerboard as described in Chapter 4.

9-10 Open-riser stairs permit the space to be unblocked, providing a view. They are also an attractive architectural feature. They are used here on a U-shaped stair.

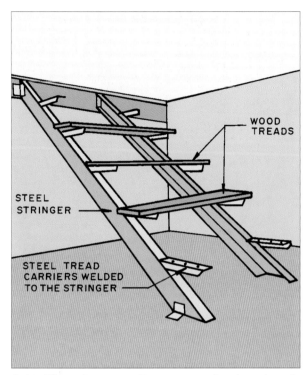

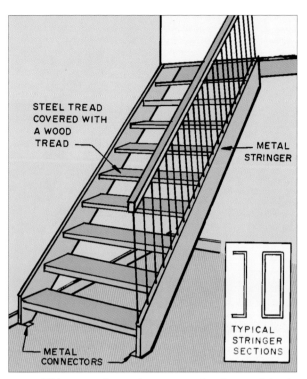

9-11 The stringers are C- or rectangular-shaped steel members. Wood treads are screwed to heavy-metal-tread carriers that are welded to the stringer.

9-12 This open-riser stair uses metal stringers. Metal treads are welded to the stringers and wood treads are screwed to the metal treads.

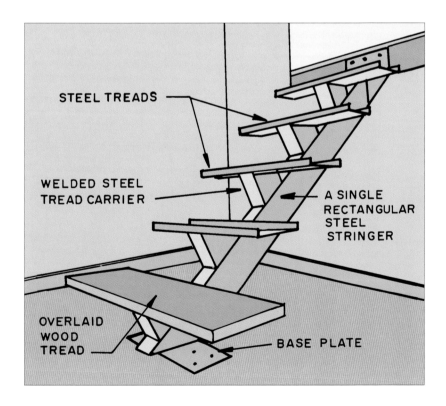

9-13 An open-riser single-stringer stair supports wood treads with heavy steel carriers and steel treads.

Another manufactured open-riser stair uses metal C-shaped or rectangular stringers. The treads are held with metal carriers welded to the stringer (**9-11**). The stair is mounted to the stairwell and floor with metal straps welded to the stringer.

Another metal-framed open-riser stair is shown in **9-12**. The stringers are metal sections. The treads are metal and are welded to the stringer. Wood treads are screwed to the metal treads.

A single-stringer open-riser stair is shown in **9-13**. It provides a dramatic appearance. The single-stringer is a steel rectangular member to which tread carriers and steel treads are welded. Wood treads are placed over the steel treads and secured to them.

BALUSTRADES

The stair manufacturer provides balustrades to complement the stair design. Some of these run the balusters to the stringer (**9-12**) and others to the tread (**9-14**).

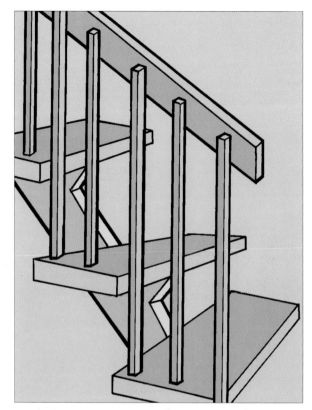

9-14 Open-riser stair manufacturers provide a variety of attractive balustrades.

Disappearing Stairs

10-1 Disappearing stairs provide an economical way to access storage space in the attic and do not permanently occupy floor space.

Courtesy Werner Ladder Company 1-724-588-2000

Disappearing stairs are used to provide access to areas that you might use for light storage and will access infrequently. They do not take up floor area and are less expensive than building a permanent stair to the area. A common location is in the ceiling of a garage over which you will use light storage. Disappearing stairs do not meet codes for access to living areas (**10-1**).

There are two basic types of disappearing stairs, folding and sliding. The folding type is in three hinged sections. The sliding type has a single stringer and slides up into the attic as a one-piece unit. Both are available in aluminum and wood as shown in **10-2** and **10-3**.

FOLDING DISAPPEARING STAIRS

The disappearing stair is hidden behind a plywood panel in the ceiling. When it is pulled down, the stair on top of it is unfolded (**10-4**). When you are finished you fold up the stair and close the panel. These stairs are available in wood and aluminum.

When you purchase a disappearing stair, examine several types. They come preassembled in standard sizes to fit into openings 22 to 30 inches wide and require a space 54 to 72 inches long. Remember that the panel opening size listed in catalogs refers to the

10-2 (Near right) This wood disappearing stair is available in several widths and has a weight, carrying capacity of 300 lbs. It has a handrail and slip-resistant treads.

10-3 (Far right) This aluminum disappearing stair is lightweight, easy to operate, and not affected by moisture. It has a weight-carrying capacity of 300 lbs. It has a handrail and slip-resistant treads.

size of the ceiling panel. The stairwell opening must be wider than this to accommodate the jambs, springs, and hardware needed to install the stair. A 22-inch-wide unit frame will fit between ceiling joists spaced 24 inches O.C. Observe the size of the rough opening specified by the manufacturer.

Disappearing stairs come with a number of labels and warnings concerning their use. To prevent accidents, these should be observed. For example, there are weight limits on what you carry on the stair. For folding stairs the typical range is from 250 to 300 lbs. The labels also give directions on proper installation.

Use these stairs with caution because they are steeper than regular stairs. Manufacturers recommend that you do not climb these stairs with something in your hands because they are so steep. To observe this safety recommendation

you need someone to help you move items up and down from the attic. You could enter the attic and have someone below hand things up to you without their climbing the stair more than a tread or two.

10-4 The folding disappearing stair has three sections that fold up on top of the ceiling panel.

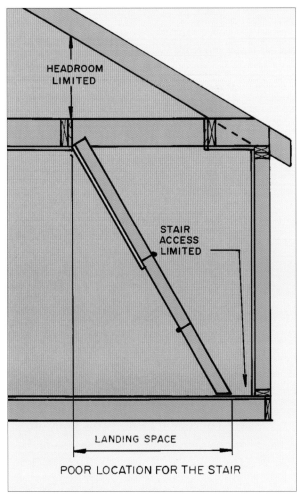

HEADROOM
LIMITED

STAIR
ACCESS
LIMITED

LANDING SPACE

POOR LOCATION FOR THE STAIR

10-5 Position the stair so you have plenty of head-room in the attic.

POSITIONING
THE STAIR

Before you order a disappearing stair measure the height from the floor to the ceiling. Stairs are available for ceiling heights from 7 feet to 10 feet 10 inches. Also check in the attic to see if the roof will give you the headroom needed to use the stair. You need as much headroom in the attic as possible. Placing the stair near the center of the house will obviously give you as much headroom as is possible (**10-5**). You also need room on the floor for the required landing space (**10-5**). In addition, room is needed between the

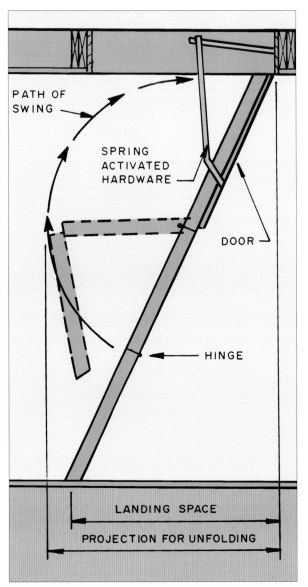

PATH OF
SWING

SPRING
ACTIVATED
HARDWARE

DOOR

HINGE

LANDING SPACE

PROJECTION FOR UNFOLDING

10-6 When locating the folding disappearing stair, leave enough room so it can fold up and swing closed at the ceiling.

end of the stair and a wall or other obstacle so you can mount the stair safely. Finally, the stair requires space so it can swing out and unfold (**10-6**); this is specified by the manufacturer.

The most commonly used disappearing stair in residential construction has three ladder-like sections. One section is secured to the plywood ceiling panel and the other two unfold (**10-7**).

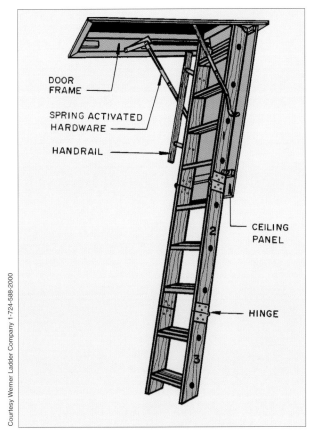

10-7 This is a typical three-section folding stair.

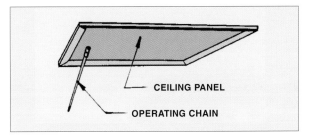

10-8 The ceiling panel is held closed by strong springs. It is opened by pulling down on the cord located on one end.

10-9 After locating the opening for the stair, cut away the wallboard.

The ceiling panel is held in the closed position by strong springs on each side. You open the panel by pulling on a cord attached to it (**10-8**). The ceiling panel swings on a piano hinge. As you lower the panel, you grasp the folded sections and pull them out and unfold them until they are in a straight position. Refer to **10-6**.

THE ROUGH
OPENING

The instructions that come with the stair will specify the size of the rough opening. The rough opening usually specified is about ½ inch wider than the actual size of the framing at the top of the stair. As you position the stair you can shim between the rough opening's framing and the stair frame.

If the stair is being installed in existing construction, locate it on the ceiling and cut away the wallboard (**10-9**). Check for clearances in the attic and the space below. After you remove the wallboard you will need to cut and reinforce the ceiling joists.

When you are cutting the opening in the ceiling, wear eye protection and a dust mask.

Measure from a fixed location and mark the approximate center of the opening. With a chisel and hammer cut through the wallboard. Enlarge the opening with a saw until you locate a joist.

From the joist locate the sides of the rough opening. Generally you place the long dimension parallel with the joist.

Cut the opening on the rough opening line. It is easiest if you cut it into several small pieces, because the material is heavy.

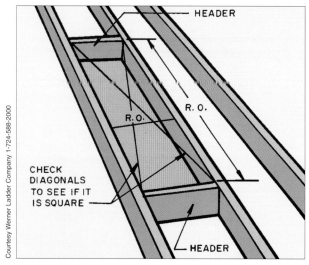

10-10 Stairs requiring a 22½ inches rough opening can fit between joists spaced 24 inches O.C. without cutting a joist.

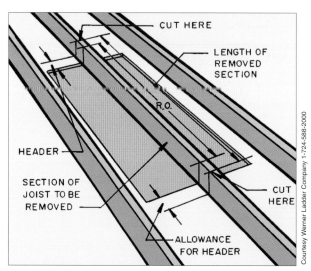

10-11 After cutting the opening, mark the joist to be cut. Remember to allow for a double header on each end.

If the stair is located parallel with the ceiling joists and they are spaced 24 inches O.C. and you use a stair requiring a 22½-inch-wide rough opening, you will not have to cut a joist. Install headers as shown in **10-10**.

Wider stairs and ceiling joists spaced 16 inches O.C. will require you to cut one joist, as shown in

10-11. After you cut the opening in the wallboard, nail a 2 × 6 to the joist to be cut and to several on each side. This holds the cut joist in place as you proceed to install the stair (**10-12**).

Cut the joist and install double headers on each end (**10-13**). Install the stringer on the side to establish the width of the rough opening (**10-14**).

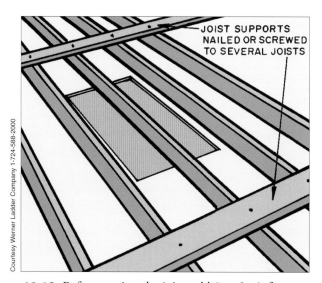

10-12 Before cutting the joist, add 2 × 6 reinforcements on each end to hold it in place. Otherwise you will probably crack the ceiling wallboard.

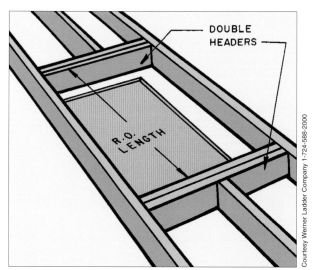

10-13 After you cut the joist, install double headers on each end.

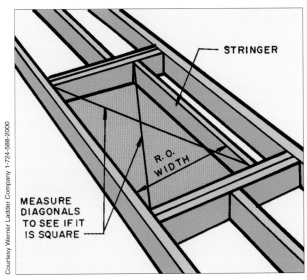

10-14 After the headers are in place, nail the stringer to set the width of the rough opening.

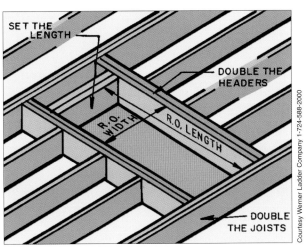

10-15 If you run the stair perpendicular to the ceiling joists, you will have to cut several joists. The ceiling will need to be supported by a beam and posts below.

If the stair is installed perpendicular to the joists, you will have to cut several as shown in **10-15**. Review Chapter 3 for information on framing stairwells. You will probably need to support the ceiling with posts below until you get the new headers in place, if this is installed as part of a remodeling job.

10-16 This is the rough framed opening from below. The temporary supports hold the stair frame in place as it is leveled and secured to the rough ceiling framing.n

Note that if your house uses roof trusses you must not cut the ceiling joists. You will have to consult with an engineer or a truss designer from a local company for advice on how you should frame the roof before cutting the ceiling joists. It is recommended that you use a stair that will fit between the joists without having to cut one of them. Your local truss manufacturer may recommend that you add a second joist alongside the original joist.

INSTALLING THE STAIR

After the rough opening is framed and the ceiling material is nailed to it, prepare temporary supports for the stair. Nail or screw a board on each end and let it project out about Á inch or as directed by the installation instructions (**10-16**). Screw these to the rough framing so they can be easily removed when the job is finished.

Now, with several helpers, raise the stair into the opening. Have several sturdy stepladders available. Keep the stair in a folded condition. Tilt it as necessary to get it through the opening. The side with the hinge must be on the side of the opening from which you want the stair to pivot. Rest the stair frame on the temporary supports. It may help if one person works from the attic to place the stair in the opening. Be certain to have some subfloor down in the attic for this person to stand upon.

Now open the ceiling panel but keep the stair folded on top of it. As you level the stair frame, secure it temporarily to the rough opening with several nails, but do not drive them home—you may need to remove them. Check the stair frame to see that it is still square You do this by measuring across the diagonals. If they are the same, it is square. Use wood shims between the stair frame and the rough opening to hold it level and square. Do not hammer the nails in too hard or you may bow the frame, causing the ladder to rub the sides

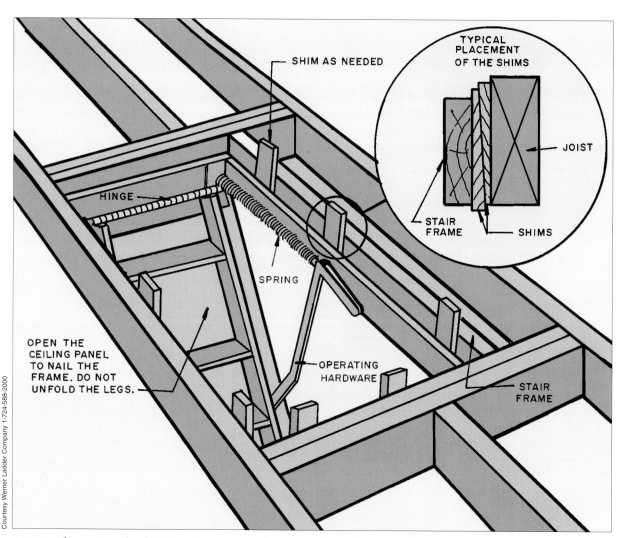

10-17 After setting the folded stair in the opening, secure it to the ceiling framing with nails or screws. You can lower the ceiling panel to give room to install the fasteners. Use wedges to keep the sides of the stair frame straight.

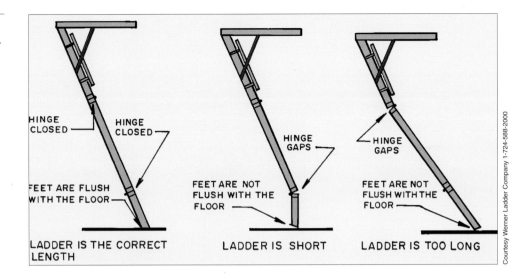

10-18 The ladder on the wood disappearing stair must have the length adjusted so that each hinged joint closes and the feet rest solidly on the floor.

HINGE CLOSED — HINGE CLOSED

FEET ARE FLUSH WITH THE FLOOR

LADDER IS THE CORRECT LENGTH

HINGE GAPS

FEET ARE NOT FLUSH WITH THE FLOOR

LADDER IS SHORT

HINGE GAPS

FEET ARE NOT FLUSH WITH THE FLOOR

LADDER IS TOO LONG

as you close the stair. Use the framing square to make certain the sides are straight (**10-17**).

Nail the sides of the stair frame to the sides of the rough opening with 16d box nails or 3-inch wood screws. Drill pilot holes through the frame for the screws if they are used. Use wood shims to fill any gap between the door frame and the sides of the rough opening. Screws will give a stronger connection and can be removed if necessary to adjust for levelness. The main hinge at the top of the stair is now screwed through the stair frame into the rough opening framing. Follow the fastening instructions provided by the manufacturer.

ADJUSTING
THE LADDER

The ladder will be extending down, touching the floor. Most likely some adjustment in its length will be needed. In **10-18** you can see that the stair with the correct-length ladder has the hinged joints closed and the feet tightly against the floor. It shows what happens if the ladder is too long or too short.

If the stair is too long, measure the distance from the floor from the bottom of the second section on the front and back of the ladder, as shown in **10-19**. It is suggested that you measure each of the legs separately because frequently the distance from the ceiling to the floor is not the same on both sides of the ladder. Mark the trim line with a sharp pencil and cut to it. Lower the third section to the floor and test it for fit.

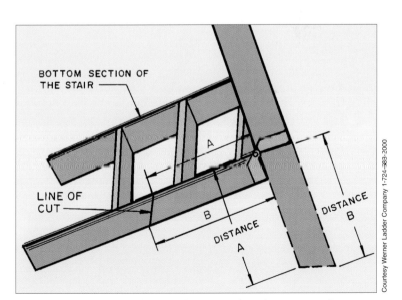

BOTTOM SECTION OF THE STAIR

LINE OF CUT

A

B

DISTANCE A

DISTANCE B

DISTANCE B

10-19 To adjust the ladder to the correct length, measure distances A nd B, lay them out on the bottom section, and cut on the line located.

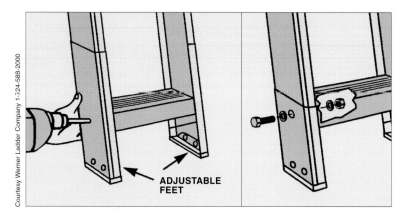

ADJUSTABLE FEET

10-20 Aluminum disappearing stair ladders have adjustable feet that are slid until the ladder is the proper length; they are then bolted to the leg.

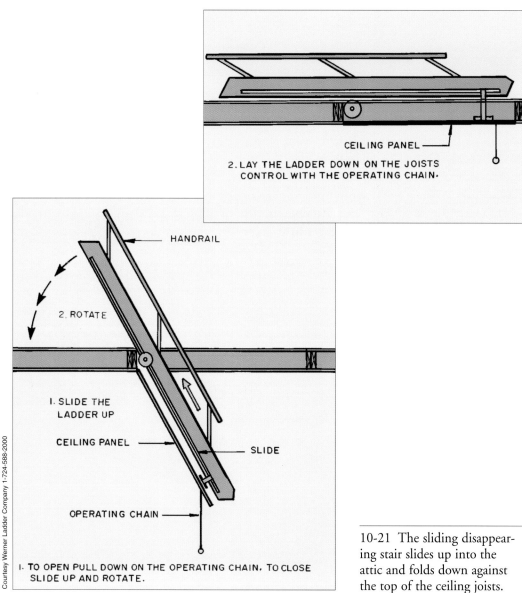

CEILING PANEL

2. LAY THE LADDER DOWN ON THE JOISTS CONTROL WITH THE OPERATING CHAIN.

HANDRAIL

2. ROTATE

1. SLIDE THE LADDER UP

CEILING PANEL

SLIDE

OPERATING CHAIN

1. TO OPEN PULL DOWN ON THE OPERATING CHAIN. TO CLOSE SLIDE UP AND ROTATE.

10-21 The sliding disappearing stair slides up into the attic and folds down against the top of the ceiling joists.

Once the stair is the correct length, fold it up and check to be certain it clears the sides of the frame in the ceiling opening.

Aluminum stairs also have to have the length adjusted. They face the same conditions shown in **10-18**, on page 153, for wood stairs. They come with adjustable feet (**10-20**). You slide the feet until the ladder is the correct length and secure it in place with bolts.

SLIDING DISAPPEARING STAIRWAYS

Sliding disappearing stairways have solid stringers. The stair slides on guide bars carried by spring-loaded cables. In the closed position the stair slides over the top of the ceiling joists and the ceiling panel (**10-21**). The stair is pulled down by pulling on a hanging cord. It then rears up into the attic and slides down the ceiling panel to the floor.

Disappearing stairways are available in the same sizes as folding stairs and have load-carrying capacities of 400 to 800 pounds. They tend to be sturdier than folding stairs (**10-22**).

Sliding disappearing stairs are installed in much the same way as folding stairs. Observe the manufacturer's detailed instructions.

10-22 A sliding disappearing stair has the ladder as a single unit. It uses special hardware to slide into the attic and fold down against the joists.

Metric Equivalents

[to the nearest mm. 0.1cm, or 0.01m]

inches	mm	cm	inches	mm	cm	inches	mm	cm
⅛	3	0.3	13	330	33.0	38	965	96.5
¼	6	0.6	14	356	35.6	39	991	99.1
⅜	10	1.0	15	381	38.1	40	1016	101.6
½	13	1.3	16	406	40.6	41	1041	104.1
⅝	16	1.6	17	432	43.2	42	1067	106.7
¾	19	1.9	18	457	45.7	43	1092	109.2
⅞	22	2.2	19	483	48.3	44	1118	111.8
1	25	2.5	20	508	50.8	45	1143	114.3
1¼	32	3.2	21	533	53.3	46	1168	116.8
1½	38	3.8	22	559	55.9	47	1194	119.4
1¾	44	4.4	23	584	58.4	48	1219	121.9
2	51	5.1	24	610	61.0	49	1245	124.5
2½	64	6.4	25	635	63.5	50	1270	127.0
3	76	7.6	26	660	66.0			
3½	89	8.9	27	686	68.6	inches	feet	m
4	102	10.2	28	711	71.1			
4½	114	11.4	29	737	73.7	12	1	0.31
5	127	12.7	30	762	76.2	24	2	0.61
6	152	15.2	31	787	78.7	36	3	0.91
7	178	17.8	32	813	81.3	48	4	1.22
8	203	20.3	33	838	83.8	60	5	1.52
9	229	22.9	34	864	86.4	72	6	1.83
10	254	25.4	35	889	88.9	84	7	2.13
11	279	27.9	36	914	91.4	96	8	2.44
12	305	30.5	37	940	94.0	108	9	2.74

Conversion Factors

1 mm	=	0.039 inch	1 inch	=	25.4 mm	mm	=	millimeter
1 m	=	3.28 feet	1 foot	=	304.8 mm	cm	=	centimeter
1 m²	=	10.8 square feet	1 square foot	=	0.09 m²	m	=	meter
						m²	=	square meter

Index

A
Angle newel, 13
Architectural woodwork, 25
Architectural Woodwork
        Institute (AWI), 25

B
Baluster-marking tool, tele-
        scoping, 120
Balusters
    cutting, 119
    definition of, 13
    designs for, 113
    space between, 10
    stepping length of square
        end, 120
Balustrade
    centerline, locating,
        102–103, 118
    closed, 100, 101, 102
    handrails, 113
    open, 4, 5
    open-riser stair, 145
    over-the-post. *See* Over-the-
        post balustrade
    post-to-post. *See* Post-to-
        post balustrade
    starting newel, installation
        of, 104–108
    terminology, 13
    variation, 126–129
Basement stairs, 7
Bore Buster, 121
Brackets, 124, 137
Building codes
    balusters, 10
    curved stairs, 96

design process and, 14–16
    handrails, 9–10
    landings, 10
    open-riser stairs, 138
    regional aspects, 14–15
    rise, 8, 15–17
    run, 8, 15–17
    slope of stairs, 10
    spiral stairways, 99
    stair width, 9

C
Carriages, 13
Ceiling joists, rough opening
        for disappearing stairs
        and, 150–151
Circular stairs, 12
Codes. *See* Building codes
Curved stairs
    codes for, 96
    design, 94–95
    installing, 94
    layout, 92–93, 94
Cutting
    balusters, 119
    housed stringers, 64–65
    mortises, 64–65, 140
    skirtboard, 44–47
    stringers, 40

D
Design process
    architectural woodwork and,
        25
    building codes and, 14–16
    drawings for, 21–24
    straight stair, 18–21

Disappearing stairs
    folding. *See* Folding disap-
        pearing stairs
    sliding, 155
Dowel screws, 117
Drawings, reading, 21–22
E
Easings
    starting, 114
    up-, over-, 114
End-cap fitting for over-the-
        post balustrade, 114

F
Finial, 136
Fittings for handrails, 114
Folding disappearing stairs
    adjusting ladder for,
        153–155
    installing, 151–153
    manufactured, types of,
        146–147
    positioning, 148–149
    rough opening for, 149–151
    warnings for, 147

G
Gooseneck
    installing, 130–131
    for over-the-post balustrades,
        114

H
Handrail
    connectors for, 123–124
    holes, boring, 121
    securing, 133

Handrails
    building codes, 9–10
    closed stair, 137
    definition of, 13
    over-the-post, 114
    profiles for, 113
Hangerboard, 41
Headroom, 19–21
Housed stairs
    assembly, 66–71
    installing assembled, 71
    wedge for, 66
Housed stringers
    cutting mortises for, 64–65
    description of, 60
    laying out, 60–66

I
I-joists, framing stairwells with,
    31–32
Installing
    assembled stair, 71
    curved stairs, 94
    folding disappearing stairs,
        151–153
    gooseneck, 130–131
    risers, 48–49
    open-riser stairs, 142
    balustrades, 115–125,
        129–136
     skirtboard, 44–47
    stringers, 41–44
    treads, 48–49
International Residential Code,
    15

J
Joist hangers, metal, 29

L
Landing newel, 13
Landings
    framing, 77–81

height of, 22, 24
requirements, 72
for straight stairs, 73–74
for U-shaped stairs, 10, 11
width of, 7, 10
Locating the Stair, 4
L-shaped stairs
    description of, 10, 11
    planning, 22–23, 74–76

M
Mechanical connectors, for
        newel post
    for concrete, 109
    freestanding, 110
    hanger bolt, 108–110
    metal angles, 111
    metal mounting palte
        112–113
    plastic mounting plate, 112
    screw anchors, 109, 112
    threaded insert, 108–109
    wood dowel fastening, 111
Metric equivalents, 156
Mitering
    skirtboard or riser, 53–54
    stringers, 55–56
Mortise
    cutting, for housed stringer,
        64–65
    stopped, for open-riser
        stairs, 140

N
Newels/newel posts
    definition of, 13
    mechanical connectors,
        108–113
    notching, 105–108
    starting, 13, 130
    starting, installation of,
        104–108
Nothced stringer stairs, 36–59

O
On-site calculations, 19
Open-riser stairs
    assembly, 141–142
    balustrades, 145
    designing, 138–139
    installing, 142
    manufactured, 142–145
    stringer layout, 139–140
    stringers, 144
    treads, 138, 139, 140
Over-the-post balustrade
    description of, 100
    installing, 129–136

P
Partitions, 20, 30–31, 42–43
Pitch block, 129
Planning, 4–13
Post-to-post balustrade
    description of, 100, 101
    installing, 115–125
Pythagorean theorem, 36–37

R
Rail bolt wrench, 123
Rise
    building codes, 8, 15–17
    for straight stair, 18–19
    total, 15, 18
    unit, 15, 18
Risers
    for carpeted stairs, 48–49
    definition of, 13
    layout for housed stringer,
        62–64
    mitering, 53–54
Rosette, 136
Run
    building codes, 8, 15–17
    for straight stair, 18–19
    total, 15, 18
    unit, 15, 18

S

Skirtboard
   balustrade centerline and, 103
   closed, 40
   cutting, 44–47
   definition of, 13
   installing, 44–47
   mitering, 53–54
Sliding disappearing stairs, 155
Slope of stairs, 4, 10
Spiral stairways
   codes for, 99
   installing, 97–99
   stairwell opening, 96, 97
Stairs
   adding to existing house, 33–35
   basement, 7
   carpeted, installing treads/risers for, 48–49
   circular, 12
   curved, 92–96
   folding disappearing. *See* Folding disappearing stairs
   housed, 66–71
   location, 4–7
   L-shaped. *See* L-shaped stairs
   manufactured, 88–91
   parts of, 12–13
   sliding disappearing, 155
   slope, 4, 10
   straight, 36
   stringer requirements, 36–38
   turning with winders, 82–87
   types, 10–12
   U-shaped. *See* U-shaped stairs
   width, 9

Stairway Manufacturers Association, 25
Stairwell
   building, 29–32
   definition of, 26
   framing with I-joists, 31–32
   length, 22, 23, 24
   L-shaped stairs, 30
   opening, 12
   straight, framing for, 26–28
   U-shaped stairs, 30
   width, 22, 23, 24
Starting newel
   definition of, 13
   height of, 130
Starting steps
   bullnoses, 56–57
   installing, 58–59
Stopped mortise, for open-riser stairs, 140
Stringers
   C-shaped, 144, 145
   cutting, 40
   dropping, 39
   housed, 60–66
   installing, 41–44
   before installing, 40
   layout, 39–40
   open-riser stairs, 138, 139–140
   for open-riser stairs, 144, 145
   rectangular, 144, 145
   requirements for straight stairs, 36–38
   right-hand & left-hand, 62
   single, for open-riser stair, 144, 145
Subfloor, 16
Subfloor-to-subfloor distance, 16, 17

T

Total rise, 15, 18
Total run, 15, 18
Traffic flow, stairway access and, 5–6
Tread bracket, 136
Treads
   for carpeted stairs, 48–49
   definition of, 13
   layout for housed stringer, 62–64
   open-riser stairs, 138, 139, 140
Turnout fittings
   for over-the-post balustrades, 114

U

Unit rise, 8, 15, 18
Unit run, 8, 15, 18
U-shaped stairs
   framing landing for, 77–81
   landing for, 10, 11, 24
   planning, 24, 74–76
   stairwell opening for, 24

V

Volutes, 114, 134

W

Wedge, 66
Width of stair, 9
Winders
   building, 85
   carpenter-built stair framing for, 86–87
   definition of, 10
   layout, 84
   usage requirements, 82–83
Wrought-iron balusters, 134, 135